Wireless Radio: A Brief History

ALSO BY LEWIS COE

The Telephone and Its
Several Inventors: A History
(McFarland, 1995)

The Telegraph: A History of Morse's Invention
and Its Predecessors in the United States
(McFarland, 1993)

Wireless Radio
A Brief History

LEWIS COE

McFarland & Company, Inc., Publishers
Jefferson, North Carolina, and London

The present work is a reprint of the library bound edition of Wireless Radio: A Brief History, *first published in 1996 by McFarland.*

LIBRARY OF CONGRESS CATALOGUING-IN-PUBLICATION DATA

Coe, Lewis, 1911–
    Wireless radio : a brief history / by Lewis Coe.
        p.   cm.
    Includes bibliographical references and index.

    ISBN 0-7864-2662-4 (softcover : 50# alk. paper) ∞

    1. Radio—History.   2. Inventors—Biography.   I. Title.
TK6547.C63   2006
621.384 — dc20   96-25734

British Library cataloguing data are available

Cover illustration ©2006 Photodisc

Manufactured in the United States of America

McFarland & Company, Inc., Publishers
  Box 611, Jefferson, North Carolina 28640
    www.mcfarlandpub.com

To the memory of Haraden Pratt, a real radio pioneer and an engineer's engineer. He was my boss in the decade before World War II. When the war was over, he said: "We might as well write off what we have been doing as history."

Acknowledgments

In preparing this book the following persons were especially helpful, providing extra effort to move the project along: Lynda Burgess of Rockwell-Collins; Elaine Cardone of the U.S. Navy; Ray A. Crockett of ITT Aerospace Communications; Bengt Dagas of Swedish Telcom; Andrew Goldstein of IEEE; Chief Hill of the U.S. Coast Guard; S. C. Houk; Colonel J. E. McCarty (AUS, retired); and Roy Rodwell of Marconi International.

In addition I must thank Lynn Frank, head of Reference Services, and her colleague Lisa Anstak, of the Crown Point (Indiana) Community Library, for their dedicated help in locating needed reference material.

Table of Contents

List of Illustrations

xi

Preface

It was a time of wonderment for a six-year-old boy living in the Kansas City of 1917. From our home on the southern outskirts of the town we took the Swope Park streetcar line when we wanted to go "downtown." We took the car downtown to see "Birth of a Nation" and in the other direction out to the Swope Park Zoo. Quite often we would see one of the open cockpit biplanes of that time soaring overhead. In those days the sound of an airplane was enough to bring people out for a look. On one of these trips I spied a home where there were some tall poles in the yard supporting a spidery network of wires. With childish curiosity I asked my mother what this was. She replied with a serious expression, "It's one of those new wireless stations." From her expression and tone of voice I concluded it was best not to ask any further questions.

After the war we moved to Galva, Henry County, Illinois. By this time radio broadcasting was commencing to emerge in its first primitive form. The only people that had radios were serious experimenters, who in many cases also operated amateur radio sending stations. One of my playmates told me of a man in town who had a radio receiving set with which he could hear voices and music over the air. My friend told me that he thought the man would be willing to let us listen to his radio. Arrangements were made at last and in due time we were ushered into the presence of this miraculous device. We put on headsets and could hear sounds of a piano playing and a man talking. We listened and listened and the time passed rapidly. It was getting dark and past supper time. I hurried home in great excitement only to be greeted by an irate mother who insisted on punctuality at meals.

Mother had cut a slender stick from the backyard cherry tree and started applying it vigorously to my bare legs as I came up the kitchen steps. "Where have you been?" she shouted. I was so keyed up that I scarcely felt the whipping and said exultantly, "Ma, I heard a radio—I heard a man talking on the radio!" This marked the beginning of my interest in radio, a subject that then had all the mystique of space exploration today.

In looking at the current radio literature I discovered that the books are either serious technical treatises or devoted to the superficial aspects of entertainment radio. Also, it was noted that radio has become mostly a generic word applied to standard broadcasting. This book is an attempt to catalog all the various uses of the radio spectrum in nontechnical terms. It is felt that the public needs a greater appreciation of what radio really is and the many ways it is used. Television, for example, is not something apart from radio, it is merely radio carrying signals which can be translated to visible pictures.

Readers with an interest in the subject of communications should consider some of the books in the bibliography. By all means read *Marconi* by Jolly and, if you can find it, a companion volume *My Father Marconi* by Degna Marconi. *The Pulse of Radar* by Sir Robert Watson-Watt has much non-technical reading that will acquaint the reader with the drama surrounding the development of radar which saved England from the German bombers and missiles.

This book will use as little technical language as possible and will not deal with the stars of entertainment radio, or the programs. Their story has already been amply told.

Lewis Coe
Spring 1996

· 1 ·

They Called It Wireless

In the beginning they called it wireless. Since previous electrical communication had been by means of wires, "wireless" seemed like the logical name and it served until 1906. In that year an international conference meeting in Berlin, Germany, decided that the word "radio" should henceforth be used to describe the new miracle of communication. Derived from the Latin *radius* (a ray, or beam of light), the new word was thought to better describe the radiation of electromagnetic waves from a central point. From force of habit the word wireless was still widely used in the early days. However, after the *Titanic* tragedy, the first legislation passed in the United States relating to this new phenomenon was called the Radio Act of 1912.

The word wireless continued to be used in England and the colonies, and still is today. In the rest of the world the term radio has long been used. Radio has become a generic word and, as popularly used by the public, it normally refers to the broadcasting services of voice and music. Yet radio correctly refers to a multitude of services besides public broadcasting. Modern technology continues to add many new uses. They are all correctly called radio. Curiously, the term wireless is being revived in connection with some of the new services. Possibly this is to draw attention to the services that might not be so spectacular if they were simply identified as radio.

The real story must begin with a young Scot named James Clerk Maxwell. Maxwell was one of those nineteenth-century geniuses who started unraveling the secrets of physics by sheer mental powers alone. Today, researchers can start with a vast store of accumulated knowledge. They have laboratory facilities that were unavailable to the most advanced institutions in Maxwell's time. Maxwell, born in 1851 in Edinburgh of a prosperous family, could have ended his days as a member of the landed gentry. Instead, he exhibited such precocity as a youth that it was apparent that he would never be comfortable with a life of ease. Instead, he was destined to unlock some of the most complicated puzzles of physics. Before he was 18 he had written scientific papers that were accepted by the most learned scholars of the time. Teaching at Cambridge, he was forced through illness to retire to his Scottish estate. While there, he was able to complete most of the work on his most important work, the book *Electricity and Magnetism*, published in 1873.

Maxwell was the first to advance the idea that there might be electromagnetic waves that were similar to light waves. This was a startling concept for the time. Many of his readers simply did not have the grasp of advanced mathematics to understand his reasoning. Although Maxwell had proved his theories mathematically, he had not performed any practical experiments.

Proof of Maxwell's theories had to wait 13 years for the work of Heinrich Hertz, a young German physicist. Hertz demonstrated in laboratory experiments that indeed there was a form of electromagnetic radiation and that it was different from anything hitherto known. Maxwell died at the early age of 48 and Hertz died when he was only 37. If these two brilliant scientists had lived a normal life span there is no telling what increased knowledge we might have had at a much earlier date. Maxwell died from cancer, so maybe nothing could have saved him. Hertz, on the other hand, died from blood poisoning caused by an infected tooth. Modern medicine could probably have saved him by routine treatment. However, even the brilliant experiments of Hertz did not seem to stir much interest in any practical application of his work. The idea of communicating through space was so novel at the time that most serious scientists did not dwell on it or even consider it.

It was not until after Hertz's death that anyone seemed to realize the potential for space communication that was embodied in the discovery of Hertzian waves. The person who was inspired by Hertz's work seemed an unlikely individual to be interested in such difficult subjects: Guglielmo Marconi, son of a well-to-do family living on an estate near Bologna, Italy. He could well have grown up and ended his days among the landed gentry, as did his father before him. But, like Maxwell, he had an inquisitive mind and could not sit idle. Marconi was on summer vacation with his mother in the Italian alps when he first got the idea for a practical communications system after reading Hertz's biography. Nothing could be done until the family returned to the estate near Bologna. Then Marconi got permission to use the upper floor of the house as a laboratory. It was necessary for him to share the space with the silkworm trays that were an important part of the farm's operations. First, he tackled the problem of duplicating Hertz's experiments. The next step involved sending signals from one end of the attic to the other. During all of this early period, Marconi only dared to hope that the same idea had not occurred to others. Next came longer-range experiments outside and much testing of different antennas and ground systems. All of this work was done with small induction coils as the source of high voltage to energize the spark gaps that generated Hertzian waves. Intelligence was transmitted by the Morse telegraph code, long used for land wire communication. When Marconi was convinced that he had the basis for a workable system for space communication, he offered his idea to the Italian government. Much to his surprise and disappointment, the government was not interested in wireless. So Marconi took his idea and equipment to England. Even though he remained a loyal Italian subject until the end of his life, Marconi's wireless became a British institution, always identified with England. Marconi was a well-educated young man and spoke English fluently. This occasioned some surprise among the newspaper men who interviewed him on his first trip to America.

Marconi's mother was a member of a prominent Irish family and she had well-placed acquaintances in England. With his mother's influence Marconi was able to gain an interview with William Preece, head of the British Post Office communication system. Once Preece had seen the original demonstrations of Marconi's equipment he realized that it was the greatest electrical invention of the nineteenth century and one that was of great value to a nation like Great Britain with far-flung colonies and a large maritime fleet. With the Post Office sponsorship, progress was rapid and demonstrations were conducted over an ever increasing range.

Marconi's arrival in England brought immediate reaction from others who claimed to have invented the same thing that he did. Chief among these was Oliver Lodge who, in fact, had duplicated Hertz's experiments. Lodge never attempted to patent his ideas for a wireless telegraph system before Marconi's arrival. Lodge was an easygoing physicist and was more interested in research than commercial exploitation. He finally applied for and was granted four British patents in 1897. Marconi had filed his application for a British patent in March 1897, only two months earlier than Lodge's application. Lodge, however, did not seem to be interested in pursuing his system for commercial purposes, while Marconi, with Post Office sponsorship, was eagerly forging ahead. Even when Lodge formed a partnership with Henry Muirhead to manufacture wireless equipment, there was not much threat to the supremacy of Marconi. The matter was finally resolved in 1911 when the Marconi Wireless Telegraph Company quietly acquired the Lodge patents and the Lodge-Muirhead syndicate was dissolved.

The coherer detecting device also caused some controversy. Coherers actually had been devised by several persons. The version that Marconi brought to England was an improvement on any then known and he claimed it as his own. Coherers were basically simple devices and formed the detecting element of all the early wireless systems. They consisted of a glass tube filled with metallic filings. When a radio signal was applied it caused the filings to stick together, or "cohere." This closed the local direct current circuit that activated a Morse sounder or printer. Once an impulse had been received, it was necessary to tap the glass tube to "decohere" the filings and make them ready for the next signal. This was an unsatisfactory system due to lack of sensitivity to weak signals and being unable to discriminate against interference. However, for a time it was the only thing available and the first results were obtained with it. Radio pioneer Robert Marriott had this to say about the coherer: "This device was publicized as wonderful, and it was wonderfully erratic and bad. It would not work when it should, and it worked overtime when it shouldn't have."

It has often been said that Marconi himself invented nothing. He simply took the laboratory artifacts of others and combined them into a workable system of communication. Early experiments involved testing communication between the mainland and the East Goodwins lightship, which was moored about 12 miles offshore. The experimental circuit was used in two separate incidents during the year of tests. The Ramsgate lifeboat was summoned by wireless to give aid to a vessel aground on the Goodwin Sands. In another incident a steamer collided with the lightship and aid was again summoned by wireless. These incidents gave early promise of the role that wireless would play in marine communications. The primitive nature of the early wireless systems sharply limited their utility but they worked well enough to give a glimpse of the future. Before wireless, ships set sail on the vast, empty stretches of the sea and nothing more was heard of them until they arrived at their distant destination. Those that didn't arrive were presumed lost with all hands. Only chance encounters with other ships offered much hope to vessels in distress.

By 1909 wireless had improved to the point where few passenger ships would leave port without it. A dramatic incident that year proved once and for all that wireless communication was an absolute necessity for ships at sea. In heavy fog a collision occurred between the White Star line *Republic* and the Italian ship *Florida*. The Marconi operator aboard the *Republic*, a young man named John Binns, was able to get his emergency wireless transmitter functioning and broadcast a call for help. The international distress signal "SOS" was not yet in widespread use so Binns called "CQD," the official Marconi distress call. The vessels had collided at a point 26 miles southwest of the Nantucket lightship. The distress calls were received at Siasconset, Nantucket Island, and that station coordinated the rescue efforts. Only four persons lost their lives in the collision and some 1,400 passengers were saved by transfer to the *Florida* and the liner *Baltic*, another ship that responded to the wireless calls. This was the first instance of wireless saving a large number of lives. Jack Binns was lionized as a hero but protested that he was merely doing his job. Nevertheless, the image of the heroic wireless operator was fixed in the public mind, only to be reinforced by John Phillips and Harold Bride of the *Titanic* approximately 3 years later.

Wireless again captured the public attention in 1910 when it led to the arrest of a Dr. Crippen who had murdered his wife in London. The newspaper accounts of the murder caught the eye of Captain Kendall, master of the liner *Montrose* bound for Quebec. He decided that two of his passengers were the escaping Crippen and his girlfriend, disguised as a boy. Scotland Yard was notified by wireless and sent a detective on a faster ship that arrived in Canada simultaneously with the *Montrose*. Crippen was found guilty and hanged. His companion, a Miss Ethel LeNeve, was acquitted.

In spite of his preoccupation with the rapidly expanding wireless enterprise, Marconi seemed to find time to engage in many romantic encounters. One notable affair was with Josephine Hulman of the prominent Indianapolis family. After a somewhat frantic transatlantic courtship they finally drifted apart. His first marriage was to Beatrice O'Brien, a well-born Irish girl who was 10 years his junior, in 1905. The marriage was soon in trouble, with Marconi neglecting his young bride to attend to business and other distractions. Once when he was returning from a business trip to America, Beatrice sought to surprise him by taking a passage on the mail boat that was going out to meet the incoming liner. She arrived in the midst of a wild shipboard party and was made to feel like an intruder. Not surprisingly, this marriage ended in divorce.

Marconi played the field for a while before marrying Christina Bezza-Scali in 1926. It was a difficult courtship for him as Miss Bezza-Scali had been raised in such a strict social regimen that she was not allowed to appear in public without a chaperon. Marconi's new wife was less than half his age, but she proved herself fully equal to the task of managing her famous husband. Before his death Marconi had discovered the reflections of high-frequency radio waves from metallic objects. If he had been able to continue research into this phenomenon, it is likely that what was later known as radar would have been available to the Axis Powers at the beginning of World War II. When Marconi died in 1937, radio stations all over the world observed a two-minute silence in his honor. *The Times* (London) on July 21, 1937, commented as follows: "What other men had been content to prove impossible, he accomplished; and this is surely greatness. The history of wireless communication has been a history of miracles; but the true miracle, as Carlyle remarked, is the life of a man — the vision and the faith, the patient labour illuminated by the unshakable resolve, which surmount all the barriers and in the end confound the wise."

Marconi's original transmitters all used the high voltage spark gap to generate Hertzian waves. The first experimental sets used induction coils with vibrating contact current interrupters to generate the high voltages required. Later, the more powerful sets used high-voltage transformers to generate the spark gap voltage. The ultimate came in the powerful transmitters such as those at the U.S. Navy's station at Arlington, Virginia. Here a 500 hertz (Hz) generator and step-up transformer was used to create the high voltage. A so-called rotary spark gap was used. The advantage of the rotary gap was that it created a higher-pitched signal and could also dissipate the high power involved. The best of the spark gap sets were impressive and served well for a number of years. They were, however, relatively inefficient and radiated a broad signal that complicated the problems encountered when a number of different stations tried to operate in close proximity. A purely local problem with high-power spark sets was the ear-splitting noise created by the spark. Spark transmitters were often placed in acoustically insulated rooms to deaden the noise. Before long it was apparent that the spark gap technology had about reached its limit. The British Marconi company was reluctant to give up the technology that had led them to the leading position in radio communication. Furthermore, at first they did not have any patent rights to use the improved methods that were starting to appear. They finally yielded to progress and one of their first modern continuous wave transmitters was a General Electric alternator transmitter used at Carnarvon, Wales, in 1921.

The first real improvement came with the arc transmitter. Carbon arcs had long been used for illuminating purposes before the invention of the incandescent lamp by Edison. For this reason they had been investigated by many inventors seeking to improve their performance and reliability. Around the turn of the century an English engineer named William Duddell discovered the principle of negative resistance in connection with the carbon arc. This meant that by adding a resonant circuit to the arc it could be made to oscillate at a frequency determined by the constants of the resonant circuit. Duddell's arc would only oscillate at audio frequencies, audible to human hearing, and it was dubbed the "singing arc."

In 1902 Valdemar Poulsen, a Danish engineer, carried Duddell's work a step further and succeeded in making the arc oscillate at the higher frequencies used in radio communication. He did this using specially designed electrodes operating in a sealed chamber, with hydrocarbon vapor, and in the presence of a strong magnetic field. The arc became the first transmitter capable of generating pure, undamped waves. It was even possible to use the arc for transmitting voice signals, although there was no good way to modulate it at high power levels. Arc transmitters were widely used at both shore stations and on ships. They were somewhat complicated to operate and were notorious for exploding when an incautious operator introduced too much alcohol into the arc chamber. Arc transmitters were brought to the United States in 1909 when Cyrus Elwell, an engineer for the Federal

Telegraph Company of California, went to Denmark and negotiated the purchase of the patent rights to the Poulsen arc (see biographies below). The unit he brought back to the United States was tiny by comparison with later units — only 100 watts — but it provided the basis for early experiments. By gradually scaling up the equipment Federal Telegraph finally produced a 30 kw unit that outperformed a powerful rotary spark transmitter at the navy's Arlington station. The navy wanted still more power and Elwell thought he could build a 60 kw unit by merely scaling up the parts again. But it didn't work. The larger unit consumed 60 kw on the input but there was no corresponding increase in output power. Obviously, more work was needed and this was finally done by Elwell's successor at Federal, an engineer named Leonard Fuller (see biographies below). Elwell himself had always been a controversial figure in spite of his obvious accomplishments. A personal acquaintance, Haraden Pratt (see biographies below), described him as "one of those individualists with whom it is hard to get along unless both parties see eye to eye."

The most powerful arc transmitters ever constructed by the Federal Telegraph Company were the 1,000 kilowatt units built for the U.S. Navy at Bordeaux, France, during World War I. But even these were eclipsed by a station that operated at Malabar, Java, from 1917 to 1927. Rated at 3,000 kw, the transmitter was normally operated at slightly less power in the range of 1,600–2,400 kw. The antenna was suspended over a mountain gorge. It should be noted that arc stations were normally rated by the input power. Assuming 50 percent efficiency, the output power was about half the rated input.

Arc transmitters were gradually eliminated when the new vacuum tube transmitters came into use. However, many were used right up to the time of World War II. Perhaps the last to be in operation on land were the point-to-point stations operated by the Mackay Radio and Telegraph Company between cities on the Pacific coast. At least one of the old high-power shore station arcs has been preserved in operating condition. It is located at Lyngby Radio Station near Copenhagen, Denmark. On May 28, 1994, the old arc transmitter was designated an electrical engineering milestone by the Institute of Electrical and Electronic Engineers (IEEE).

One of the early pioneers in the conversion from spark gap transmitters to continuous wave transmitters was Reginald Fessenden (see biographies below). He was a leader in developing new detecting devices to replace the early coherers, which were characterized by a lack of sensitivity and not being suited to continuous wave reception. Fessenden was without question one of the geniuses of early radio, but his personal characteristics left much to be desired. Erratic in temperament and not very successful in the business applications of radio, he was a difficult man to work for or with. One of his remarks to a subordinate was typical: "Don't try to think. You haven't got the brains for it!" Fessenden was awarded the Institute of Radio Engineers Medal of Honor in 1921. Unfortunately, he had heard that when Marconi won the same medal earlier it was described as being of solid gold. He had his own medal analyzed and discovered that it wasn't pure gold. In a rage he returned the medal to the IRE and asked that his name be taken off the list of Medal of Honor winners. After a close friend, G. W. Pickard, made an investigation and determined that both medals were exactly the same composition, Fessenden agreed to take his back.

Trained in alternating current theory, Fessenden correctly considered radio waves as being merely an extension of the lower-frequency alternating current voltages used in power circuits. His solution for a transmitter was simply to build an alternating current generator that would produce frequencies high enough to radiate from an antenna and thus be useful for communication. This was a simplistic approach and theoretically correct. The problem lay in constructing such a machine. Fessenden knew that the General Electric Company was the leading builder of electrical machines in the United States and persuaded them to accept his order for an alternator. General Electric assigned a young Swedish engineer named Ernst Alexanderson (see biographies below) to work on the project. Alexanderson's experience had been confined mostly to rotating electrical machinery and he was really not familiar with radio. Referring to the alternator project he once said, "It was an invention I had to make in order to hold my job."

Although Fessenden and Alexanderson had many disagreements before the design was complete, an alternator was eventually delivered to Fessenden. With the small alternator installed at his Brant Rock, Massachusetts, station, Fessenden commenced a period of active experimentation. Initially, a report was received that test signals from the low-powered alternator at Brant Rock had been heard in Scotland. On Christmas Eve, 1906, Fessenden made a broadcast in voice and music from Brant Rock using the alternator. This may have been the first transmission of anything other than Morse code signals and it was heard by ship radio operators along the Atlantic coast.

All of the early radio work was primarily concentrated on radiotelegraphy. This was what was needed to augment ocean cables, provide auxiliary links to existing landlines, and to fill the need for communication with ships at sea. Even so, the great dream was to transmit the human voice and music over the airwaves. The first attempts involved using the spark gap transmitters. These attempts were unsatisfactory due to the nature of the radio waves generated by spark sets. With the advent of arc and alternator transmitters the experiments were a little more successful. These transmitters emitted a pure, undamped wave just like the vacuum tube oscillators that came later. The only problem was that there was no satisfactory way of modulating the wave except on low-power sets. Some microphones used on the larger arc sets had to be water cooled to prevent them from overheating. Fessenden's 1906 broadcast from Brant Rock using his low-power alternator was one of the first transmissions of voice and music, but there were several others at about the same time. Oddly enough, none of these early experiments envisioned anything like public broadcasting that came along a few years later. Rather, they were concerned with using voice channels instead of telegraphy for point-to-point radio communication, and the telephone company at the time took considerable interest in these experiments because they could see possible applications to augment wire lines.

Real progress in voice communication had to await the coming of the vacuum tube oscillator as a generator of undamped waves. The same tubes that generated the carrier wave could also be used as amplifiers to increase voice levels from the microphone. Once tubes of sufficient power rating became available it was possible to build effective radiotelephone transmitters of any desired power. Lee De Forest (see biographies below) invented the three-element vacuum tube in 1906, and this was the beginning of the new technology for generating and receiving radio waves either for telegraphy or telephony. De Forest's original tube, which he called the "audion," was a small glass bulb containing a filament, a grid, and a plate. The remarkable thing about it was that changes of potential on the grid effected larger variations in the current flowing from the plate to the filament. By introducing some coupling between the plate and grid called "feedback," the tube became an oscillator. As the tubes were scaled up in size they could be used to generate radio frequency power at any desired level. Also, when used as a detector in a radio receiver, the principle of feedback caused an enormous increase in sensitivity to incoming signals. It was De Forest's audion, modified to become an effective amplifier of telephone signals, that was used in the repeaters on the transcontinental telephone line when it was opened in 1915. Without the De Forest tubes, there is no way the transcontinental line could have worked. The limits had already been reached with line loading and large conductors.

One of the early scientists with a remarkable perception for the future of electrical communication was William Crookes. The Crookes tube was the forerunner of X-ray tubes, and it was only one on a long list of Crookes's inventions. Early in his career he recognized the importance of the radio frequency spectrum. He said that light rays, which most people could see, were only the tip of the iceberg in relation to the vast spectrum that could propagate electric waves through space. Crookes characterized the spectrum as a vast continent, whose resources were still unknown. He theorized that it was very unlikely that the spectrum did not contain means for communication. He wrote in the *Fortnightly Review* in February 1892 as follows:

> Rays of light will not pierce through a wall; nor, as we know only too well, through a London fog. But the electrical vibrations of a yard or more in wavelength of which I have spoken will easily pierce such mediums, which to them will be transparent. Here, then, is revealed the bewildering possibility of telegraphy without wires, posts, cables, or any of our present costly appliances. Granted a few reasonable postulates, the whole thing comes well within the realms of possible fulfillment....
>
> Any two friends living within the radius of sensibility of their receiving instruments, having first decided on their special wavelength and attuned their respective instruments to mutual receptivity, could thus communicate as long and as often as they pleased by timing the impulses to produce long and short intervals in the ordinary Morse code. I assume here that the progress of discovery would give instruments capable of adjustment by turning a screw or altering the length of a wire, so as to become receptive of wavelengths of any preconcerted length. Thus, when adjusted to fifty yards, the transmitter might emit, and the receiver respond to, rays varying between forty-five and fifty-five yards, and be silent to all others. Considering that there would be the whole range of waves to choose from, varying from a few feet to several thousand miles, there would be sufficient secrecy; for curiosity the most inveterate would surely recoil from the task of passing in review all the millions of possible wavelengths on the remote chance of ultimately hitting on the particular wavelength employed by the friends whose correspondence he wished to tap.

For 1892 Crookes's predictions were remarkably accurate. Of course, he couldn't have possibly visualized the modern scanner, which does exactly what he describes in searching for signals of unknown frequency. Even with modern equipment however, it is not easy to find an unknown signal unless the listener has some idea in what part of the spectrum it may exist. Under modern conditions, radio transmissions are anything but secret unless the messages are encoded or transmitted with the new digital systems, which are virtually undecipherable by any listener not having access to the protocol being used. The vast radio frequency spectrum, which in Crookes's time was unknown and unused, now teems with activity. Only by the strictest government regulations and international agreements is the utility of the spectrum preserved. Otherwise, it would only be a jumble of signals of no use to anyone.

The radio frequency spectrum is defined as the range of wavelengths or frequencies that will propagate through space. In the early days of radio it was common to define a channel in terms of wavelength. These wavelenghts were measured by resonant circuits with adjusting dials calibrated in meters. This was a comparatively inaccurate system, but it sufficed in the days when accurate measurements as required by modern conditions were not necessary. As the spectrum became more crowded it was necessary to start defining channels in terms of frequencies. The use of frequency instead of wavelength was first suggested by the U.S. Bureau of Standards at the second National Radio Conference, which met in March 1923.

The relationship between wavelength and frequency is governed by the velocity of light: 300,000 kilometers per second. To obtain frequency when the wavelength is given, divide 300,000 by the wavelength in meters. For example, a wavelength of 100 meters is equivalent to a frequency of 3,000 kilohertz per second. The lower limit of the radio spectrum is normally considered to be 10 kilohertz. This equals a wavelength of 30,000 meters or about 18.6 miles. Obviously, a very large antenna is required for effective radiation of such low frequencies. The previous unit of frequency measurement was cycles per second. In the 1960s this was changed to hertz to honor Heinrich Hertz. The two terms are identical in meaning.

Marconi's early work was largely based on the earlier demonstrations of Hertz. Researchers who have visited the Hertz laboratory have had the opportunity to make actual physical measurements using some of the surviving Hertz laboratory equipment. From this they have been able to conclude that Hertz used wavelengths ranging from 1.5 to 10 meters. Marconi's apparatus essentially started out using these wavelengths, although at that time no one had more than a rough idea of what wavelength they were actually using. There was no established theory of propagation and early workers used mostly the cut and try method to see what worked the best. With the short wavelengths he used at first, Marconi was working essentially with waves that were limited to line-of-sight transmission. In the process of trying anything that would increase the range he started using higher and higher vertical antennas. Since the wavelength of his apparatus was determined primarily by the resonant frequency of the antenna, he was unwittingly moving to longer and longer wavelengths. As he gradually got to the longer waves the range started to increase dramatically. The waves were now following the curvature of the earth. The theory of reflection of short waves from an ionized layer of gas surrounding the earth was not brought forth until 1902 by Oliver Heaviside in England and Arthur Kennelly in the United States. It was only natural for Marconi to pursue the methods that brought steadily increasing ranges. Large, tall antennas and lots of power was the formula that worked and it was followed for several years. Marconi did not even know at first that propagation on the waves he was using was better when the path between transmitter and receiver was in darkness. Considering the crude nature of his early apparatus and the fact that he worked often in daylight, some of his distance records are remarkable.

When vacuum tube apparatus became available, it was possible to refine the frequency measuring process. Heterodyne oscillators could be tuned to zero beat with an incoming signal and the frequency could be measured with an accuracy unknown in the old wave meter days. Broadcast stations now use frequency monitors that enable the station to keep within 20 hertz or less of the assigned frequency. Frequency counters, using transistors and numerical readouts, now count the actual number of hertz in the incoming signal and display it directly. This is a far cry from the days when one read an analogue dial as accurately as possible and then consulted a calibration chart to determine the frequency.

The first accurate control of frequency came with the discovery of the piezoelectric properties of quartz crystals. Quartz plates cut to a certain thickness had a natural period of vibration when subjected to an electrical impulse. This was the favorite method of controlling transmitter frequencies up to the time of World War II. Some military transmitters of that period required large crystal kits containing dozens of crystals just to tune the equipment to the various tactical frequencies that might be required. Now solid-state digital technology has taken over and frequencies of any desired value can be generated synthetically and be quickly called up by punching buttons. Quartz crystals still find a considerable amount of use, especially in low-cost consumer type of equipment where they are actually cheaper than the synthesized frequency generating circuits. Even the synthesized circuits sometimes incorporate a quartz crystal to generate a reference frequency.

• 2 •

Marine Radio

On the night of December 1, 1976, the Liberian freighter M/V *Melias* was steadily making her way across the vast reaches of the Gulf of Mexico, bound from Guyana to Tampico, Mexico. Shortly after midnight the quiet routine of the ship was interrupted when an excited crewman summoned the captain and told him that the hull was leaking badly. The captain did not hesitate long before telling the radio operator to send the distress message. At 0050 GMT (6:50 P.M. CST), listeners in the Midwest heard fragments of the message on 500 kHz, the international distress frequency. The fragments that were received gave the first notice of the desperate emergency that was taking place 300 miles from Tampico and 600 miles southwest of New Orleans.

Calmly spelled out in Morse code were the words "immediate assistance" and "hold flood." The distress message was received by NMG, the Coast Guard station at New Orleans, and they in turn retransmitted the message as follows:

> DDD SOS SOS SOS DDD CQ de NMG 01 0235 GMT M/V
> *Melias*/5MEK posn 23.09N 93.24W taking on water possible danger
> of sinking vessel can remain afloat 3 to 4 hours posn 23.09N 93.24W
> any vessels in vicinity are requested to assist if possible advise U.S.
> Coast Guard New Orleans/NMG

At 0305 GMT another message was heard direct from the ship, "require immediate assistance ship is sinking." Meanwhile, NMG had sent the auto-alarm signal. This activates automatic receivers on all ships within range, even if the radio operator is off duty. Many ships responded to the call but unfortunately all of them were too far away. The position of the *Melias* was out of the regular shipping lanes and incidentally was over one of the deepest spots in the Gulf of Mexico.

The 311 feet *Melias* went down about 1400 GMT. The last message from

the ship read: "We are abandoning. The ship is sinking and breaking up."
Three hours later the Greek vessel *Ageis Sonic* arrived at the scene and all 25
seamen from the *Melias* were rescued from the lifeboats and rafts. When the
distress message was first received at New Orleans, Coast Guard fliers went
into action and headed out over the dark waters of the Gulf. They found the
sinking ship and dropped life rafts in case they were needed. The Coast
Guard men that headed out that night probably thought of the old Coast
Guard motto: "You have to go but you don't have to come back!" The sinking of the *Melias* was a classic tragedy of the sea in which radio made the
vital difference for the men on board. The rescue was due to the operation
of the 500 kHz distress signal system that had been in operation since the
early days of radio.

Radio operators have maintained their heroic tradition ever since the
days of Jack Binns of the *Republic* and Phillips and Bride of the *Titanic*. On
November 22, 1994, the Cypriot Coal Carrier *Polydoros* was reported burning in the Atlantic. All of the crew members were rescued by a U.S. Coast
Guard heliocopter except the radio officer, Hepolito Elango. He was found
slumped over the wireless key, dead from smoke inhalation after sending the
SOS that brought help to his crew mates. A monument to radio operators
who lost their lives at sea is maintained in Battery Park, New York. The
sponsoring organization is the Veteran Wireless Operators Association. Most
recently, the following names were affixed to the monument: "Serhiy B. Bukov,
Radio Officer, SS *Salvador Allende*, Atlantic Ocean, December 9, 1994"; "Hepolito Elanga, Radio Officer, SS *Polydoros*, Atlantic Ocean, November 22, 1994";
and "Olexander V. Lagno, Chief Radio Officer, SS *Salvador Allende*, Atlantic
Ocean, December 9, 1994."

For a radio operator, hearing the SOS signal is an experience never forgotten. Most operators might spend years at sea without ever hearing it. This
situation was to change during the submarine warfare of World War II when
it was not uncommon to hear a distress call every night. The signal SOS was
adapted at the Berlin international radio conference in 1906. The letters were
selected merely because they were distinct when spelled out in Morse code.
They did not stand for "save our souls" as popularly supposed by the public.
The earlier distress signal CQD had been officially designated by the Marconi company in their General Order Circular No. 57, dated January 7, 1904.
The signal was derived from "CQ," the general call to all stations, and "D"
for distress. It did not stand for "Come Quick Danger" as was popularly supposed.

A victim of the curious government mentality that cuts budgets for
essential services and lavishes money on doubtful projects, the Federal Communications Commission (FCC) has had to cut back many of its former field
operations. It still stands guard, however, and is ready to prosecute flagrant

violators of the radio laws. One sure way to get the FCC's attention is to send a false distress signal. The people who send such signals are in the same class with those who shout "fire" in a crowded theater or drop cement blocks from highway overpasses. In 1993 a Fairfax, Virginia, amateur radio operator was found guilty of sending false distress signals on 14.313 MHz. The distress calls described a sinking vessel off the Turks and Caicos Islands in the West Indies with six people in the water and needing immediate help. The distress calls activated a full-scale search by the U.S. Coast Guard and patrol craft were also sent out by the government of the Turks and Caicos. This search cost the Coast Guard $100,000. A plea-bargaining settlement resulted in the amateur being required to surrender his station and operator license and dispose of his radio equipment. In addition, he was ordered to pay $50,000 to the Coast Guard.

When the *Titanic* met her tragic fate on April 15, 1912, radio operators Phillips and Bride at first sent the call CQD. Then they decided to use SOS as well. The nearby *Californian*, only 20 miles away, did not hear the calls because her radio operator was not on duty. The deck officers of the *Californian* saw the rockets being fired from the *Titanic* and notified their captain. The captain elected to disregard the rockets, even though he could have ordered his radio operator to find out what the trouble was. It thus happened that the *Carpathia* was the only ship to hear the distress signals and give effective assistance. Even the *Carpathia* might have missed the call except for the fact that her radio operator had continued to listen after his watch had ended.

After the living survivors had been picked up by the *Carpathia*, other ships hastened to the area to pick up bodies. Among these was the cable ship *Mackay Bennett*, which was in port at Halifax. Many bodies were found floating in life jackets, perfectly preserved due to the cold water. The bodies were stacked up like cord wood on the decks of the rescue ships and embalmers did their grim work while ambulances waited on the docks.

The *Titanic* tragedy had the immediate effect of revising regulations for radio operations at sea. Vessels were required to maintain a continuous radio watch on the distress frequency of 500 kHz; minimum qualifications for radio operators were established in the form of licenses; and iceberg patrol was established to report dangerous conditions by radio.

After the first legislation in 1912 that laid down the rules for radio equipment on board ship, many passengers were lulled into a false sense of security. They thought that if the ship was radio equipped, there would be nothing to fear in an emergency. Unfortunately, some shipowners played fast and loose with the new rules. Radio inspectors found ships that were about to embark on a long ocean voyage with radio equipment that was not in working order. In 1914 there was a great deal of publicity when two ships, the SS *Majestic* and the SS *Cedric*, were not permitted to sail because of faulty radio equipment. An editorial appearing in *Electrical World* of February 7, 1914, stated: "The sublime confidence of the seagoing public in wireless as an all-patent saviour would appear to be misplaced. It is high time that all passenger steamers were equipped with emergency or auxiliary transmitters which are really worthy of the name." Safety became the all-important issue. Never again would a ship be allowed to sail without adequate lifeboats for all the passengers. The investigation into the *Titanic* disaster had disclosed that there were only about half the number of lifeboats needed to carry the passengers and crew.

But poor judgment on the part of ship captains has caused many tragic sinkings at sea, even though the radio system was functioning perfectly. This is due to the fact that a radio operator cannot send a distress message without the specific order of the master.

When the *Vestris* was enroute from New York to South America in 1928, the vessel sprang a leak in the hull. The captain thought he could make port and save the ship. Even after the vessel developed a 30-degree list the captain stubbornly refused to call for help. By the time the captain changed his mind, the ship was lost and the passengers and crew took to the boats. Over 100 lives were lost, including Radio Officer O'Loughlin. One young couple enroute to a new job in South America had a harrowing experience. They had ended up in different lifeboats that were picked up by two different ships and taken to different ports. Not for some time did either one know that their loved one was safe.

In October 1934 the steamer *Morro Castle* caught fire off the New Jersey coast. The three radio operators on board repeatedly asked the captain for permission to send the distress signal. When permission was finally granted Chief Radio Operator Rogers had to sit with his feet on the chair rungs as the steel deck was becoming too hot. The vessel was finally towed ashore but not until at least 100 lives had been lost. Captains in these kinds of cases are apparently obsessed with the idea that they will be censured for losing a valuable ship or having to pay salvage charges for being towed to shore.

It has happened that coastal station operators have heard a call for help, only to have the signals suddenly disappear. In the vast expanses of the Pacific this has usually meant the complete loss of a vessel and all the persons on board. Before radio, many ships disappeared in this way. Only a chance encounter with another ship offered much hope of survival in the days before radio. And even chance encounters did not guarantee a safe rescue.

When the *Great Eastern* was on her second Atlantic crossing in 1861, a severe storm was encountered. The ship suffered heavy damage, the most serious of which was the loss of the steering gear. Then the brig *Magnet* appeared in response to the rockets being fired from the *Great Eastern*. This brought a ray of hope to the passengers before it was realized that the little ship could not save more than a handful of the 832 persons on the larger ship. Realizing that there was nothing else to do, the *Magnet* finally left, but not before one of the *Great Eastern* passengers callously offered to buy the brig and cargo just to save his own skin. The captain of the *Magnet* was no fool; he probably realized that once the individual making the offer was ashore he would conveniently forget all about buying the boat. The *Great Eastern* finally made a return to port with a jury-rigged steering gear. Without radio, even the owners did not know what was going on. The big iron ship, then the largest vessel afloat, survived many other misadventures before finding her useful role as a pioneer cable-laying ship in 1865–66.

The basic distress signal system that came into being after the *Titanic* disaster functioned well for many years. But gradually the basic character of shipping started to change. No longer did dozens of huge passenger liners ply the main routes to Europe, South America, and Asia. Even though ship's radio operators were not highly paid as a class, they were deemed an expensive luxury by shipowners. This was especially true for freighters where there were only a handful of crew on board, compared to the hundreds of persons carried on the former ocean liners. It was finally decided to replace the old system with an automated service, made possible by the new satellite technology.

In 1993 the U.S. Coast Guard discontinued its continual monitoring of the distress frequency 500 kHz, a practice dating from 1905. Many ships and coastal stations still monitor 500 kHz, but the basic tool for distress calls is now the Global Maritime Distress and Safety System, GMDSS. Typical of the inexplicable logic that sometimes characterizes government agencies was the action of the Coast Guard after terminating their Morse code monitoring. After discontinuing this monitoring, they immediately advertised for private contractors to bid on supplying essentially the same service. Old-time radio operators have had reservations about the new automated system. Humans, they feel, can often deal better than robots with complicated situations. Most ships will still carry radio officers, although they are primarily needed as maintenance technicians for the electronic equipment. Marine radio operator licenses still have a Morse code requirement. Eventually, this may disappear as all communication with ships becomes automated.

Before radio, ships were navigated across the oceans by methods that had really not changed much since the time of Columbus. Deck officers took regular noon sightings on the sun. These sightings determined local noon time, and by comparing with the ship's chronometer the longitude was determined. Latitude was determined by measuring the altitude above the horizon of the various heavenly bodies. Navigation by this method could be quite accurate, yet it was severely impaired if there were extended periods of cloudy weather that made sky observations impossible. At such times it was necessary to run by dead reckoning, using the magnetic compass to indicate the direction and the patent log to measure the ship's speed. Perhaps the first application of radio to navigation was the radio direction finder. Direction finders took advantage of the directional effects of a loop antenna. Loop antennas were merely large coils of wire strung on a frame and arranged on a pivoting mount so they could be rotated in a full circle. The loop antenna when tuned to a distant transmitter gave two indications, a maximum and a minimum signal. Of these, the minimum was the more distinct response. A compass in connection with the loop indicated the direction of the distant station. A typical application was to take bearings on two shore stations some distance apart. Plotting these bearings on a chart gave a triangular pattern that indicated the position of the ship. These direction finders became standard equipment on every oceangoing ship and were used for many years.

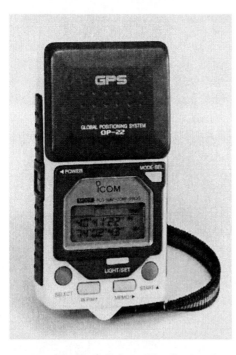

2.1. Hand held global positioning receiver (photo courtesy of Icom of America).

Later equipment included the Loran and Omega systems that transmitted powerful coded signals that determined position. After World War II, radar added another capability, particularly for short-range location of other ships and shore hazards. With satellite technology has come perhaps the most sensational aid to navigation. The Global Positioning System (GPS) receives signals from satellites and prints out the exact position directly in latitude and longitude (see photo 2.1). Many of these systems are accurate to 100 meters or less and they work whether the sky is cloudy or clear. Gone are the old sightings and laborious calculations that were the terror of young officers

2.2. Ship's radio console, installed as a unit on many World War II freighters (photo courtesy Mackay Radio).

qualifying for their first license. Even small private craft can utilize the new technology. Simplified handheld units are now available and affordable to anyone who can afford a small boat.

Radio ended the old isolation of ocean voyages, not only from a safety angle but in the ability of passengers to receive the latest news and keep in touch with business or social acquaintances. Most of the large ocean liners published daily newspapers during the voyage, with the latest news received by radio. The larger liners were virtually floating cities. A large percentage of the passengers were people who had active business and social lives. As a result, they sent and received many radio messages during a long ocean voyage (see photos 2.2, 2.3). Coastal stations were established at strategic positions that gave the closest access to incoming and outgoing ships. These stations were kept busy on a 24-hour basis handling the telegraph traffic to and from the ships.

Most of the early traffic was handled in Morse code at manual speeds

2.3. Radio room of the British merchant ship *Himalaya* about 1955 (photo courtesy of the Marconi International Marine Communications Co., Ltd.).

of 25 or 30 words per minute. Some of the larger ships eventually began to use automatic equipment capable of much higher speeds to handle the huge volume of messages that were filed. Now there are few passenger liners on long ocean voyages and message traffic is handled by teleprinters working through satellites. Smaller ships still use radio telegraphy to send and receive messages to and from shore stations. Operation now is on the shortwave or high-frequency channels instead of the old system of exclusively using longwave, low-frequency channels.

Coastal stations are much fewer in number now and some are even automated so that one operator controls more than one station. This is a cost-cutting method that is justified by the greatly reduced volume of message traffic. On freighters, which constitute the majority of oceangoing ships today, there are a few routine messages exchanged with the ship's agents when arriving at a port and that is about all. On passenger vessels radiotelephone service is usually available and this further reduces the volume of telegraph traffic to be handled.

Active users of radio communication are the large fleet of tow boats that move barge traffic on the inland waterways. Although called tow boats, these craft do not actually tow anything. Instead, they push the barges, often in large groups tied together with steel cables. Originally, these river boats carried radio operators who sent and received Morse code messages just like their oceangoing brethren. Then improved radio telephone equipment made it possible to discontinue Morse code operations. The captain and officers could operate the radio equipment with a minimum of technical knowledge. The modern tow boat is equipped with single sideband radio equipment for operation on the high-frequency bands that have a range of several hundred miles day or night. For short-range communication a VHF radio using FM is carried. The crew working out on the barges can talk to the pilot house with handheld units. The FM sets also carry on the all-important communications with the various locks that a tow boat must pass at frequent intervals.

The boats also carry radar, which is of great assistance in navigating on a river where the hazards are never far away. In addition to the other radio facilities, the boats have access to public telephone service supplied by repeater stations located at strategic points on the waterways. Private pleasure craft have also traditionally used the mobile radio telephone service operating on the VHF marine channels. However, it appears that this VHF service will be superseded by a satellite telephone service in the not too distant future.

The modern boats bear little resemblance to the old steamboats that Mark Twain made famous. No longer does a crew member have to take soundings for shallow water and the cry "Mark Twain" is heard no more. Instead, electronic depth finders automatically display the depth of water and indicate the reading on the wheelhouse instruments. Crews live in comfortable quarters while on board and work rotating tours of duty, giving them time ashore at regular intervals. One of the problems that has been encountered with crews on tow boats are the new laws prohibiting sex discrimination in hiring. Why a woman would want to be locked up on a boat with a crew of 24 roughneck crewmen is a question best left to the imagination.

Traditionally, the only woman on a tow boat was the cook, and she was provided with her own private quarters. One boat captain agonized when he heard that a girl had been assigned to his boat: "What am I going to do with her? She can't bunk in the men's quarters and if I try to move her in with the cook the cook will quit!" Folks along the river normally think of tow boat officers as pretty glamorous people. One pilot heading upstream on the Ohio spied a farm lad on a big tractor in a field near the river. The pilot called another nearby boat on the radio and said, "That's where I would like to be." Chances are that the farm lad watching the powerful boat heading upstream with 6,000 horsepower and a string of 24 barges was thinking: "Boy that would be neat to run a boat like that!"

During Prohibition days, rum running flourished on the East coast of the United States. Small schooners came north from the Caribbean area and lay offshore with their illicit cargo. High-powered speed boats came out from the shore to offload the liquor. Older residents of eastern Long Island, New York, have recalled hearing the sounds of the speed boats on dark nights, sometimes mingled with the rat-a-tat of automatic weapons fire as federal agents attempted to intercept the liquor boats. The whole rum-running operation had to be coordinated by radio. Unemployed radio operators, willing to do anything to get a job, often yielded to the temptation to earn high wages on the rum-running schooners. Some were caught and sentenced to terms in federal prisons. One rum-runner operator, becoming bored while his ship lay offshore for hours at a time, decided to say hello to his buddy whom he knew was on duty at a legal shore station nearby. The rum runner tuned up his transmitter on the international calling frequency and boldly said: "Hello Joe, this is Whitey!" A dead silence followed this transmission as the shore station operator dared not be caught communicating with an illegal rum runner.

One of the best-known coastal stations on the West coast is KFS, San Francisco. Operators at the KFS marine station were sworn in to the U.S. Coast Guard for the duration of World War II. When the Philippines fell to the Japanese, the Mackay Radio commercial radio circuit to Manila was shut down and the civilian personnel of the Mackay facility in Manila were interned for the duration. One of the Mackay staff, a man named George Gould, who didn't want to be interned, managed to escape to the jungle and join a band of guerrillas.

In late August 1942 KFS operators began hearing some strange signals on the high-frequency bands used for marine communication. It sounded like someone was trying to get a transmitter going. Later on a strange signal was heard calling WAR and signing KAA. WAR is an army call and KAA was the call of the former RCA station in Manila. Since the army station did not hear KAA, he sent a blind message telling them to call KFS, a station that was hearing them.

Two-way communication was soon established and KAA sent the following message: "This is George Gould we are a bunch of guerrillas in the mountains of Northern Luzon we have a breadboard transmitter and receiver which we carry on our back. The Japanese are mostly in the cities and along the coast but there are places along the northern coast where it would be safe for a sub to land we need everything we want smokes but our direst need are shoes."

This was one of the first guerrilla messages to come out of the Philippines after the Japanese occupation. The military had authorized these radio contacts but insisted on very careful questioning to assure the authenticity of the signals. Other guerrilla units also got on the air and their activities were instrumental in driving the Japanese out of the Philippines. George Gould survived his guerrilla adventures and turned up at Mackay Radio headquarters in New York in 1945.

• 3 •

The Broadcast Boom

When radio technology progressed from Morse code to voice transmission, the stage was set for one of the greatest national crazes ever to hit the United States. Pioneer experiments by early workers using arc or alternator transmitters introduced listeners to something other than the telegraphy they expected to hear in their earphones. These early transmissions were heard only by a select few: professional wireless operators and amateur enthusiasts. Some of these transmissions had been made as early as 1905. Among the pioneer broadcasters was Lee De Forest, who set up a station in the Bronx, New York, in 1916. Typical of the casual nature of early broadcasts was De Forest's broadcast of the Wilson-Hughes presidential election on November 7, 1916. The station signed off the air at 11 P.M. with the announcement that Hughes had won!

The real broadcast boom seems to date from October 17, 1919, when Frank Conrad started sending voice and music over his amateur station 8XK in the Pittsburgh, Pennsylvania, area. Among the early broadcasts were the presidential election returns in 1920. Conrad was an employee of Westinghouse Electric Company and the company vice president Harry Davis was impressed by the enthusiasm that had been expressed over Conrad's programs. It finally became apparent to Westinghouse that there was a ready market for radio receiving sets if they could supply program material that would interest listeners. Thus was born KDKA, the pioneer broadcasting station that became a landmark for early listeners. KDKA had a strong signal that could be heard throughout the United States under nighttime conditions. Another early station, which began operating on August 20, 1920, was 8MK, a station that later became WWJ of Detroit, Michigan. Despite the primitive nature of most receivers, long-distance reception was possible because there were few stations to cause interference.

To fully understand the enthusiasm with which broadcasting was received by the public one must consider the social conditions existing in America at that time. In the large rural areas farmers were living under about the same conditions that prevailed in Civil War days. It was still primarily a horse drawn economy. A great many families did not own an automobile, and those that did could only use them in the summer months. Open cars with no heat were not much fun in winter and the wretched roads were almost impossible to negotiate during certain seasons. Few farms had electricity and were dependent solely on oil lamps for nighttime illumination. A typical evening for a farm family was to gather around the kitchen table and read by the yellowish lamplight. A few families might enjoy the luxury of an Aladdin kerosene lamp, which gave a brilliant white light compared to the old wick-type lamps.

Newspapers, the Sears Roebuck catalogue, and possibly the *Youth's Companion* for the children were typical reading matter. Trips to town were usually no more than weekly, and the movies were just getting off the ground with black and white silent pictures. The new rural telephones offered some contact with the outside world, but many farms did not even have those. Phonographs offered some entertainment to those who had them, and there was usually someone in the family who could play the piano or other musical instrument. City dwellers did not fare much better. They might have electric light and access to theaters and concerts, yet these sources of entertainment were not always affordable to the average family.

When Herbert Hoover addressed the first National Radio Conference in 1922, he said in his opening statement:

> We have witnessed in the last four or five months one of the astounding things that has come under my observation of American life. This Department estimates that today more than 600,000 (one estimate being 1 million) persons possess wireless telephone receiving sets, whereas there were less than 50,000 such sets a year ago. We are indeed today upon the threshold of a new means of widespread communication of intelligence that has the most profound importance from the point of view of public education and public welfare.

Broadcasting opened up new vistas for isolated families and quickly became the standard source of spare-time entertainment. Starting with KDKA, radio stations started springing up all across the country, faster, in fact, than government regulation could bring some semblance of order to what was becoming a chaotic situation. Stations more or less picked their own frequency and went on the air with whatever power level they could afford (see photo 3.3). Some had as little as 5 watts, little more than converted amateur stations. The Radio Act of 1927 brought the first real sense of order to broadcasting, after several years that were wild and interesting. The realization had grown that, unless the radio spectrum was utilized in an orderly manner, the new medium would shortly be useless to everyone.

In 1916 David Sarnoff, who started as an office boy with American Marconi and rose to be head of RCA, had advanced the idea of a radio music box. Demonstrating his remarkable powers of foreseeing the future, Sarnoff described his idea as a piece of equipment "which would receive several different wavelengths at the throw of a switch and be supplied with amplifying tubes and a loudspeaking telephone, all of which can be mounted neatly in a box." Sarnoff's idea was regarded as visionary in the extreme and the First World War soon had all manufacturers busy with war work. Sarnoff's business judgment was later vindicated when RCA grossed $83 million in home receiver sales during the 1922–24 period.

Since manufactured receivers were relatively expensive, millions of listeners built their own equipment. Parts supply companies proliferated and their products were sold in all manner of stores, including drug, department, and ten-cent stores. Magazines such as Gernsback's *Radio News* printed construction articles for the eager builders. A few well-heeled persons either bought the commercial sets that started to appear on the market or hired an "expert" to build a set for them. Regardless of wealth or age, almost everyone could acquire some kind of radio and most people did. With no more than a pair of earphones, a galena crystal detector, and a coil wound on an oatmeal box signals could be heard (see photo 3.2). Of course, the set had to be connected to an outside antenna, just the same as the vastly more expensive sets using vacuum tubes.

Acquiring a radio in the early days was not just the simple matter of taking it out of the box and plugging it in. First, a suitable outdoor antenna had to be erected if the listener was more than a few miles from the transmitter. Many of the sets used an automotive type 6 volt storage battery to supply voltage to the tube filaments. Since these batteries were rough on carpets or polished floors, a suitable place had to be provided for them and some arrangement had to be made to recharge the battery when it ran down. Earphone listening was standard at first; families had multiple sets of earphones so everyone could listen at once (see photo 3.1). The first sets were all battery operated and both the 6 volt "A" battery and a "B" battery were required. The "B" batteries were usually in blocks of 45 volts made up of small dry cells. Usually 90 to 135 volts of "B" was required. These "B" batteries could not be recharged, so when exhausted they had to be replaced at considerable expense. Many of the early receivers, particularly the home-built ones, were of the regenerative type. Regeneration was the controlled feedback of the detector tube, invented at about the same time by De Forest and Edwin Armstrong (see biographies below). It was the only way that the sensitivity of a simple receiver could be improved. Unfortunately, if the regeneration level was too high the detector tube went into oscillation and became a miniature transmitter. Coupled to the outdoor antennas used in

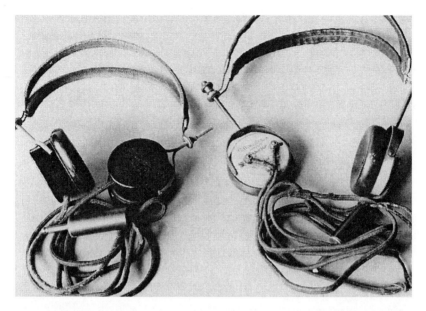

3.1. Baldwin Type E (left) at $20 and Brandes Superior at $7 were popular headphones in the 1920s (photo by Lewis Coe).

the early days, one of these oscillating receivers could be heard at some distance. This created havoc in metropolitan neighborhoods where dozens of receivers might be tuned to the same program.

For this reason, regenerative receivers were declared illegal in England. They were never outlawed here in the United States, but gradually disappeared as more satisfactory receivers were developed. The English — despite having license fees to pay and other restrictive rules — were as enthusiastic radio listeners as their cousins in the United States. The measure of British enthusiasm can be realized by looking at the license records. The number of known licensees was around 200,000 in 1923 and showed a steady rise until it reached over 10 million in 1946.

When the user of a regenerative receiver tuned in a station, he often heard a whistle. Even today, when the movies depict someone tuning in a radio, a whistle will be heard on the sound track. No radio in the last 50 years has given out a whistle when tuning in a station, yet the movies cling to this myth.

Operating practices have changed in the broadcast industry. Originally, it was necessary to have a licensed radiotelephone operator on duty at the transmitter during the hours that the station was on the air. As transmitter technology improved, it became possible to operate a broadcast transmitter by remote control, all functions of the transmitter being controlled from

3.2. Compact crystal detector receiver for headphone reception of broadcast stations (photo by
Lewis Coe).

the central studio. Now, the only requirement is that the person actually doing work on the transmitter should have an FCC license. The transmitter site is only visited when there is a breakdown or when routine maintenance is required.

Radio opened up new vistas of the outside world, producing an almost fanatical interest on the part of the public. Oddly enough, most early listeners were not so much interested in program content as they were in logging distant stations. KDKA with its relatively powerful transmitter and clear channel could be heard pretty well throughout the Eastern half of the country at night. Listeners soon found out what Marconi had learned years earlier: that nighttime conditions were better on the frequencies then in exclusive use. Listeners in rural areas had the best chance of hearing distant stations. In metropolitan areas, where local transmitters were in operation, it was almost impossible to hear distant stations. Catering to the listeners, the local stations sometimes held "silent nights," shutting down their transmitters for a given period so that the local receivers could tune in distant stations.

The idea of paid commercials was slow to materialize. Of course, most of the stations were put on the air by business firms who were not bashful about informing the public as to who they were. KDKA started out as a scheme to sell Westinghouse radio receivers. Even David Sarnoff—certainly a man geared to making money — resisted the idea of paid commercials for a long time. He thought that radio should be devoted to the education and entertainment of the public. This was a high and worthy purpose but it neglected the problem of who was going to pay for the broadcasts. A few wealthy corporations could afford to underwrite stations so that they would not have to run paid commercials to support the broadcasts. Increasingly, however, it was found that broadcasting could not flourish without a source of income. Sarnoff finally came to this conclusion himself. The alternative

3.3. Five watt (left) and 50 watt tubes, typical of those used in low powered broadcast stations of the 1920s (photo by Lewis Coe).

to paid commercial advertising would have been a tax and licensing of receivers as was done in Europe. This idea was never popular in the United States. Here it was deemed that everyone had a right to own a receiver and listen at no cost, with the commercials paying the bills. This method also made many radio stations highly profitable to the owners.

Even before commercials there were many stations sponsored by organizations that wanted to be identified with the new craze. A landmark station in the Midwest was WOC in Davenport, Iowa. WOC sported a 5 kw Western Electric transmitter and never failed to call attention to its owner, the Palmer School of Chiropractic. Dr. B. J. Palmer, the owner of the station, was a scholar and world traveler. He gave weekly lectures over WOC setting forth his opinion on various subjects.

KTNT, "Know the Naked Truth," in Muscatine, Iowa, was owned by Norman Baker, a flamboyant gentleman who was the manufacturer of a musical instrument called the Caliaphone. The instrument was a hybrid of a pipe organ and a calliope. KTNT could readily be identified by the Caliaphone music broadcast daily. Radio was made to order for a superhuckster like Baker. He bamboozled the city of Muscatine into furnishing free electricity, water, and tax exemption for his station, boasting: "I'll lift

Muscatine from a little burg lost in the Mississippi corn fields, to a city the whole world knows about." With a powerful transmitter located on a high hill, KTNT became one of the dominant stations in the Midwest. Baker had discovered the great publicity value of attacking everything from corrupt city fathers to the evils of cooking in aluminum pots and pans. Aluminum cooking utensils were then new, and alleged by some to cause food poisoning.

If Baker had stopped then, he would have been home free as a successful businessman and a flamboyant, but legal, radio broadcaster. Unfortunately, the dark side of his nature took over when he conceived the idea of establishing a cancer cure hospital. Cancer research was in its infancy at that time. When cancer victims heard Baker say on the radio that he could cure them, they took it to be true and flocked to the hospital in great numbers. For a time the venture thrived. The influx of patients benefited the local economy and Baker was regarded as a leading citizen of Muscatine.

Inevitably, the awful truth finally came out: Baker's claims of a cancer cure were completely false. This was a strange irony for a man whose radio station call letters stood for "Know the Naked Truth." In 1932 he lost a suit brought by the American Medical Association that alleged libelous statements. His empire was crumbling rapidly and he finally had to leave town under cover of darkness, loading his hospital equipment aboard a special train. Attempting to set up the hospital at Eureka, Arkansas, Baker ran afoul of the law and ended up spending four years in the federal penitentiary at Fort Leavenworth, Kansas. Emerging from prison a broken man, Baker still managed a touch of class. He spent the final years of his life living on board a palatial yacht in Miami, Florida.

Early broadcasting seemed to attract the medical quacks. It offered the means to reach large numbers of prospects at relatively low cost. Also, the mere idea of hearing of something on the radio tended to convey a certain authenticity to the product. In the tiny town of Milford, Kansas, Dr. John Brinkley used his station, KFKB, to promote his medical theories and peddle nostrums that were widely condemned by the medical profession. Among Brinkley's ideas was the transplantation of goat glands to humans to restore youth and vitality. Brinkley's downfall was brought about when he disregarded radio laws and lost his broadcasting license. He refused to give up his profitable enterprise and moved across the Texas border into Mexico. From there he could beam a powerful signal into the United States and avoid U.S. regulations.

Early broadcasting stations often evolved primarily through the enthusiasm of a few individuals, possibly through a desire to get involved with the new medium rather than with any clear idea or purpose. Such was the case with WFBM of Indianapolis, Indiana. A group of technicians who maintained the carrier current system of the Indiana Electric Company discovered that the company had a spare carrier current transmitter in storage. Carrier current is widely used by electric utility companies. It permits radio waves to be channeled along the same wires that carry electric power. This provides voice communication between stations without the expense of extra telephone wires. The carrier current transmitters of that day were practically identical to the transmitters used for public broadcasting. This gave the technicians the idea to use the spare transmitter for a broadcasting station. They took the idea to company officials and persuaded them to go along. Thus was born WFBM, a station that made its debut by broadcasting the Coolidge/Davis presidential election returns in 1924.

Early radios were viewed as electrical instruments and no attempt was made to conceal their function. For this reason radios were often located in side rooms of the home, not considered to be elegant enough for the parlor. Later in the broadcast boom the sets were designed to look like pieces of fine furniture and could be exhibited with pride in the living room. By the late 1920s the equipment operation had been changed from battery to the normal household electrical outlet. This was a lot simpler than the former array of batteries, even though connection to an outside antenna was still usually required. Listening habits had changed too. Few listeners now were looking for distance; they just wanted good, consistent reception of their favorite programs. Most programs were now sponsored by a commercial advertiser and network broadcasting made it possible to produce shows using top talent in the big-city studios and send it all over the country simultaneously. Although many of the programs had the sound of extemporaneous acting, they were not. Every word was normally read from a prepared manuscript by skilled actors.

In the days before World War II television was seen as being just around the corner. Radio manufacturers sensed that many buyers of new radios might hesitate to invest in a new radio with television imminent. The manufacturers conceived a great ploy to counter this problem. They advertised that their sets were "television ready." This was supposed to assure the potential buyer that his new radio would not be obsolete when television came in. Most of these television ready sets merely had a jack so that the sound amplifier of the receiver could be used to amplify the television sound. However, there is no record that any radio was ever used in this way.

Network broadcasting was slow to come along because of the position taken by the telephone company. They felt that transmission of the human voice for the benefit of the public was their exclusive right. AT&T owned radio station WEAF in New York and gave every indication that they were in the broadcast business to stay. The telephone company would not lease to NBC the high-grade audio lines required to interconnect stations. The

3.4. NBC studios in Hollywood, California, 1939 (photo by Lewis Coe).

only other lines available were a few copper wire, voice-grade lines owned by Postal Telegraph. Postal had built the lines originally to use the Gray harmonic telegraph system. When the Gray system proved impractical, Postal used the lines to establish a limited long-distance telephone service. These Postal lines were never much of a threat to AT&T, but they did play a part in early broadcasting. The impasse between NBC and AT&T was finally broken by skillful negotiating. In the process, WEAF was sold to NBC and the telephone company agreed to stay out of radio broadcasting (photo 3.4). Furthermore, the long-distance lines were now available to interconnect broadcast stations in any desired configuration. The first network program to celebrate the new order was held in January 1927 and joined 25 stations, reaching as far west as Kansas City. The following year the first coast-to-coast hookup came into operation.

Network broadcasting became an important part of operations for the long-lines division of AT&T. Lines had to be especially equalized for distortion-free transmission of radio programs. Only the most skilled, senior employees were assigned to handle the network lines. The precision and split-second timing required made it a stressful job, sometimes characterized as the "ulcer department" by employees. For many years employees of the AT&T long-lines department were required to be qualified Morse telegraph operators. The "order wires" between stations were Morse telegraph circuits. This was because in the early years of open-wire transmission lines, voice circuits were too valuable to be tied up with company traffic. A Morse telegraph circuit could be derived from each pair of telephone wires. As the telephone company increased the number of circuits available, the system of Morse order wires was gradually discontinued. This created a bonanza for collectors of telegraph instruments as large quantities of surplus AT&T telegraph material hit the market.

A curious offshoot of legitimate, legal broadcasting is found in the so-called pirate radio stations. There have been attempts to operate stations on board ships moored in international waters off the U.S. coast. In 1933 a Panamanian ship attempted to set up shop off the California coast. The operation raised a storm of protest, not only from the U.S. authorities but also from legal broadcasters on the 815 kHz channel that the ship had appropriated. This pirate operation was short-lived and the ship itself was towed into Los Angeles Harbor in August 1933, its broadcasting days definitely over. The FCC has maintained a stiff attitude toward offshore broadcasting. They claim jurisdiction of the stations, even though the ship may be technically in international waters beyond the 12 mile limit. As late as 1973 the radio laws were challenged again when a station on board an old minesweeper vessel was anchored off Cape May, New Jersey. This station was only on the air for 10 hours. The powerful transmitter was putting out so much heat that it set the vessel on fire. A financial crisis loomed for the owners of the station and they never attempted to return to the air. No one was charged in the incident and the Supreme Court never had the chance to rule on the legality of such operations.

Of an entirely different nature are today's pirate stations. They operate with relatively low power in the high frequency bands, typically 6,410 kHz. Using mostly converted amateur equipment, these stations broadcast on very intermittent schedules. The program content is varied, from pop music to dissertations on whatever cause appeals to the proprietor. The operators are mostly juveniles who seem to get some pleasure from what they do. It would seem that legal amateur operation would be a better alternative. Perhaps they are like the phone freaks who delight in circumventing telephone company procedures. Due to their intermittent operation, low power, and the propagation characteristics of the frequencies employed, these illegal pirates are seldom caught. However, if they are too persistent they will be apprehended and some have gone to prison as a result.

International shortwave broadcasting became popular about the time of World War II and continued through the years of the cold war. The first stations were intended to carry the message of freedom to countries behind the iron curtain. Using high power and directional antennas, these stations could pretty much target a certain area. One of the early ones was the Voice of America (VOA) station operated by the Columbia Broadcasting System in Brentwood, New York. The location was leased from the Mackay Radio and Telegraph Company and occupied space in the same building used by Mackay for its international radio telegraph station. In more recent years the VOA has operated a powerful station in Bethany, Ohio. Now, Bethany is closed down and the trend seems to be to locate medium-frequency, standard broadcast stations near the air target area. International broadcasting today seems to be more the province of various religious groups and they operate some very powerful stations in South America. Radio Australia is a landmark on the shortwave bands and beams many programs to the United States.

The period immediately after World War II was marked by a pent-up consumer demand for all types of manufactured products. Among these were radio receiving sets. Television was still not a reality for most consumers, but everybody wanted a new radio. The prewar manufacturers of radios had all geared up to military production and so couldn't immediately revert to their normal peacetime operations. Several enterprising manufacturers sought to meet the needs of consumers and make some money in the process. It was almost the original broadcast boom all over again. Elaborate manufacturing facilities were not needed to manufacturer radios: a few assembly tables and soldering irons was about all that was required.

One of the companies that sprang up to meet the postwar need was Midland Manufacturing Company (no relation to the present Midland brand of Japanese radios). Midland had enjoyed a lucrative contract during the war as a manufacturer of folding radar targets that were carried on lifeboats to facilitate rescue of crew members after the many submarine sinkings of cargo ships. The only legacy of this enterprise was some industrial sewing machines, a basic labor pool of female workers, and a venerable old two-story building in a small town in northern Iowa (see photo 3.5).

The only industrial experience possessed by many of the ladies in the labor pool was time spent in the chicken-processing plant, which had previously been the town's only industry. The chicken-processing plant, on one of the main roads entering town, could easily be identified. There were always a few chickens wandering around on the roof of the plant, no doubt hoping to escape the fate that awaited them below. Could these former chicken pluckers be taught to assemble radios? That was the question before the technical staff of Midland as they assembled to plan the new operation.

The new product was to be a five-tube table model radio of the AC-DC type in a wooden cabinet. A pilot model was available and the first step was

3.5. Radio chassis ready to be assembled in cabinets. Midland Mfg. Co. 1946 (photo by Lewis Coe).

to analyze it for mass production. This was done by identifying each individual operation necessary to build the set. Broken down to the smallest operation, assembly steps were written out on 3 x 5 file cards and might read "solder a yellow wire from terminal 4 on socket B-5 to terminal 5 on socket B-6." An individual card was considered to be what a girl could perform without holding up the production line. About 50 assembly positions were laid out on long work tables. Each position had a soldering iron and supplies of the parts needed at that particular location. Bottlenecks were sure to develop as some girls completed their operation quickly and the sets started to pile up ahead of a slower worker. In such cases the cards could be redistributed to equalize the work.

After a few training sessions to acquaint the workers with the process, it was time to make a test run of the production line. The basic sheet-metal chassis was supplied by an outside source. The first step was to rivet on the tube sockets and other parts. This was done before the chassis was placed on the production line. It was a tense moment when the first chassis was handed to the girl at the beginning of the line. Slowly the test unit passed down the line. Finally, the last girl soldered on a line cord and passed the

chassis to the test room.
Much to everyone's sur-
prise and relief, the first
set worked. From then
on it was a matter of
refining the process until
the little production line
was capable of grinding
out 500 radios a day. The
test room was staffed
with male technicians
who had radio experi-
ence of some kind. Their
job was to take the sets
as they came off the
assembly line, attach test
leads, and calibrate the
receivers with the stan-
dard test signals.

A separate assem-
bly group installed the
radio chassis into the
wooden cabinets and
attached the tuning
knobs. The last opera-
tion before placing the

3.6. Typical postcard of the "broadcast boom" era.

radio in its shipping carton was to perform a "playing radio test." " This was
to ensure that the set hadn't been damaged since leaving the test department.
Much grief was encountered in the cabinet department due to the metal
chassis mounting holes not aligning with the predrilled wooden cabinet, so
tedious refitting was often required before the chassis would fit the cabinet.

One thing that was quickly learned by the supervisory staff was that if
a worker was given a specific job he would figure out quickly the easiest and
quickest way to do it. Such was the case with the dial cord stringing operation. Many radios of the period used a thin cord looped around pulleys to
move the tuning elements of the set. Stringing these cords could be tricky,
and if it was not done right the tuning didn't work. It turned out that the
deft hands of a female quickly mastered the routine and it was one of the
least troublesome problems on the line. More serious were bad solder joints
that could occur at almost all of the line stations. Soldering was a basically
simple operation and the experienced operator instinctively knew when the
joint was correctly soldered. New operators had to learn however, and it took

a while before some of them became efficient. One bad soldered joint can keep the radio from working. Good soldering was essential and required the constant vigilance of line supervisors.

Starting up a mass production line is an unforgettable experience for those who are doing it the first time. Probably the greatest worry is to ensure that adequate quantities of parts are available. One missing part shuts down the whole line. Little Midland required 2,500 vacuum tubes a day to maintain full production. As the end of the first year of production approached, there was increasing difficulty in securing the necessary quantities of parts. This was because the major established companies were getting back into peacetime production. The parts suppliers were not about to alienate their large customers of prewar days. This left Midland in a desperate position at times. Occasionally, they had to resort to purchasing parts such as volume controls through retail channels instead of directly from the manufacturer. Another problem was the need to introduce new models at the end of the first year of production. Several variations of the original model had already been made. Included were sets for operation on 32 volts direct current from farm power plants. At that time there were still many farms in the far reaches of the plains states that did not have commercial electric power. The 32 volt models were intended for operation on the 32 volt Delco electric systems used on such farms. Since these farm radios only had 32 volts on the tubes instead of the normal 135–150 volts they were relatively insensitive.

One advantage of the assembly-card system was that to change models it was merely necessary to put up a new set of cards and supply the correct parts at the stations where they would be required. But after a year of production Midland quietly disappeared. The combined factors of parts supply, lack of financing for a new model, and increased competition from the established companies were just too much for the small company to handle. However, on some remote farm in Iowa or Minnesota it is quite possible that a Midland radio is still playing today.

•4•

Amateur Radio

When news of Marconi's discoveries started to circulate around the world, a new class of electrical experimenters appeared. The early wireless sets were simple in nature and could be duplicated by almost any competent home builder. There had always been amateur enthusiasts for electrical devices. They built backyard telegraph and telephone lines, did electroplating, gave shocks to unsuspecting friends, and in general experimented with everything electrical.

Wireless was made to order for this group of citizens. Soon they were happily communicating across town with their Ford ignition coil transmitters and galena crystal receivers. A lucky boy might have received a gift of a wireless telegraph outfit, made by Gilbert of Erector Set fame. These were kits that had to be assembled by the recipient.

The amateurs, as they were soon dubbed, followed commercial developments as closely as the available knowledge and their pocketbooks would permit. Soon some pretty impressive installations were appearing in private homes for no other purpose than the pleasure of the owners. Lofty antenna systems, precariously erected in backyards were fed by well-designed and well-built rotary spark transmitters. Especially coveted were the synchronous rotary gap transmitters. By driving the rotary gap with a synchronous motor a distinctive musical quality was imparted to the signal. Those who possessed these distinctive signals were highly envied by their brethren who did not have them.

All of the foregoing took place before voice transmission was even considered possible, and before vacuum tubes were generally available to the amateur operators. In addition, it all took place before there was any form of government regulation of radio. The amateur stations chose their own call letters and there was no such thing as requiring a license to operate. Commercial stations were operating under the same lack of regulation. In the coastal areas, where most of the commercial stations were located, the ether was often crowded with an absolute bedlam of signals, all trying to communicate with somebody. The commercial stations with their powerful transmitters could pretty well wipe out the amateurs. However, when it came time for the commercial station to switch over to the receive mode, nearby amateur signals completely blocked the commercial receiver. It was not unheard of for commercial stations to politely ask the amateur operator to stand by until the commercial messages could be cleared. Sometimes the amateurs would not cooperate and the language that passed between stations was far from polite.

Clearly, something had to be done. Commercial interests were making large investments in wireless communication and they could not function if they were routinely subject to random interference by amateurs and by each other. Probably the one single incident that sparked the first radio regulations was the tragedy of the *Titanic* in 1912. The Radio Act of 1912, for the first time assigned regular working channels for the services then in existence. Licenses were issued for stations and operators were required to have licenses attesting to their ability and knowledge of radio regulations. Since the huge loss of life on the *Titanic* had been in part due to failure of nearby ships to hear her calls for help, due to radio operators being off duty, new rules were laid down for maintaining a continuous radio watch.

At that time the part of the radio spectrum lower than 200 meters in wavelength (1,500 kHz) was considered worthless for commercial use. The great Marconi had pretty much proved that. Amateurs of the time were not too happy with the 1912 law. They perceived it as a means of putting them off the air for good. Later events were to prove that the below 200 meter restriction was the best thing that ever happened to amateur radio. With nothing to lose, amateurs started working on the shorter wavelengths and were soon achieving spectacular results with low-power transmitters and modest antenna systems (see photo 4.1).

Writing in the January 1932 issue of the IRE *Proceedings*, Professor Ernest Merritt of Cornell University declared as follows:

> Since the amateurs were not allowed to use the longer waves they went ahead with undiminished enthusiasm to get what results they could with the wavelengths assigned to them. Presumably most of them were not familiar with the theoretical reasons for believing that work with short waves was not likely to prove successful; at any rate such knowledge of theory as they had did not deter them from trying experiments which the experienced radio engineer would have regarded as foredoomed to failure. When such experiments led to success with 100 meter waves they tried 50 meter waves and found the results still better. Gradually the wavelength was reduced still further until with a wavelength of about 20 meters it was found possible to signal over distances greater than had ever before been reached, and this with only a fraction of the power used by the long wave stations.

4.1. Typical amateur radio station of 1930. "Entertainment center" at right uses Atwater Kent Model 20 receiver and homemade audio amplifier (photo by Lewis Coe).

The long-wave systems that Marconi had built were dependable and furnishing good communications, but they had reached the limit of development. With transmitters running as high as 1,000 kw of power, there was not much room for improvement by increasing power. Marconi and other commercial interests were quick to take note of the results that amateurs were getting on the shorter wavelengths. Marconi himself finally admitted he had probably followed the wrong path in the beginning. Speaking to the Institute of Radio Engineers in 1927 he said, "I admit that I am responsible for the adopting of long waves for long-distance communication. Everyone followed me in building stations hundreds of times more powerful than would have been necessary had short waves been used. Now, I have realized my mistake."

The first National Radio Conference was called in Washington by the secretary of commerce, Herbert Hoover, February 27–March 2, 1922. Represented at the conference were the industry giants, AT&T, General Electric, Western Electric, Westinghouse Electric and Manufacturing, and the Radio Corporation of America. Amateur representatives and independent broadcasting and manufacturing interests were on the other side of the table. The press had propagandized that the big five hoped to eliminate amateur radio. Secretary Hoover gave a strong rebuttal when opening the conference:

I would like to say at once that anyone starting any such suggestion that this conference proposes or had any notion of limiting the area of amateur work was simply fabricating. There has never been any suggestion of the kind, never any discussion of the subject in any shape or form. The amateurs asked to be represented in the conference and they are represented here today, and the starting of that sort of information is one of the most treacherous things that can be done. So I wish to sit on that right at the start — that the whole sense of this conference has been to protect and encourage the amateur in every possible direction.

One item to come out of the 1922 conference was to define an amateur radio operator: "An amateur is one who operates a radio station, transmitting or receiving, or both, without pay or personal gain, merely for personal interest or in connection with an organization of like interest." This has always been the preferred definition. The term "ham" came along later, apparently derived from other uses of the word ham such as ham actor. Unfortunately, the word ham has caught on and is often the word used by the general public today.

Coinciding with the emergence of amateur radio was a class of hobbyists who were only interested in listening to the early broadcasting stations. These listeners, soon to be labeled "BCLs" (broadcast listeners), had no transmitters and they keenly resented the interference by amateur transmitters (see photo 4.2). There was plenty of interference because amateur spark transmitters emitted a broad signal and the first receivers had little ability to reject strong local signals. In the days of spark transmitters, amateur operators often instituted cooperative agreements among themselves so that everybody would have a chance to operate without interfering signals. Interestingly enough, such cooperation still exists today. Amateurs have set up their own frequency governing plans for operation on the VHF and UHF portions of the spectrum, where high-powered repeater stations would create hopeless interference if the frequencies were not carefully assigned.

The friction between amateurs and BCLs was to continue for many years. The root causes began to diminish as amateur transmitters became more sophisticated and BCL receivers were better designed. Even so, as late as World War II, a high-powered amateur radiotelephone transmitter could interfere with broadcast reception in a good-sized town. This was especially true if the town was some distance from major broadcast stations. When television came along, the whole interference problem surfaced again, but this time it was of a different technical nature. Most amateur transmitters had to be redesigned to eliminate spurious radiation of the high-frequency harmonics that fell right in the new television channels.

4.2. Replica of 1929 amateur transmitter uses 210 tube in Hartley oscillator circuit (photo by Lewis Coe).

The beginning of the television era saw more and more amateurs using commercially built equipment that had been carefully designed to eliminate interference with television receivers. For the most part, amateurs have tried to cooperate with listeners in preventing interference, even though in many cases the fault lay with the receiver not the transmitter. Amateurs have always had to defer to other services that were deemed more important. Early amateur licenses often had restrictions on operating during the hours of local church services. In coastal areas restrictions were often in effect to guard against interference with vital maritime traffic. Today, amateurs operate pretty much in harmony with their neighbors, be they broadcast listeners, television viewers, or any of the host of commercial radio services.

Although amateurs have always had a subordinate position in relation to other services, they are still regarded as important by almost all regulatory bodies. In the early days of wireless, amateurs constituted a large reserve of operators with some proficiency in the Morse code and technical matters. In World War I the telegraphic ability was very important, as most communications were by Morse code. The code ability continued to be important in World War II, even though other types of communication were becoming more prevalent. Even without the code ability, amateurs constitute a large reserve of people with some knowledge of electronics. Such people are more easily trained to be a part of military communications than those who have no knowledge in such matters.

The Morse code requirement has caused some persons to label the amateurs as an elitist group. Actually, most people can master the code. Far from being an elitist group, amateur radio enthusiasts are probably the most democratic hobbyists we have. Open to all, and regardless of race, religion, or social position, all that is necessary for membership is qualification for the operating license. Amateur licenses are issued in several grades, ranging from novice to extra class. As might be expected, the higher grades are the most difficult to obtain and confer greater operating privileges. The Morse code requirement has long been a stumbling block for those who wish to operate radiotelephone sets and not use code. The code requirement continues to exist because it is a matter of international treaty. The United States already issues a no-code license for operation on the higher-frequency bands used for domestic communication. For operation on the lower frequencies, which are used for international communications, Morse code proficiency may be required for some time to come.

Amateur radio probably should be called an avocation rather than a hobby due to its recognition by the government and the fact that some kind of government license is required to participate. Like everything else, amateur radio has become more expensive. In the beginning most amateur outfits were home built, and some of them were equal to anything being used by the professionals of the day. The tendency toward home construction was enhanced by the fact that prior to World War II there was not much available in the way of commercial equipment. After the war, state-of-the-art equipment had to be designed to minimize interference with television and other radio services. Single sideband telephony became standard and precise indications of operating frequency had to be provided.

This all meant that home construction was no longer practical for most operators. Even for those who had the necessary technical knowledge, it was generally cheaper to buy a manufactured outfit. It was the old story of trying to build an automobile by buying the component parts. There were a few individuals who built state-of-the-art equipment merely because of the technical challenge it presented. For operators who had no interest in code communication, getting on the air was mainly buying a commercially built radio and just plugging it in. These individuals were soon called "appliance operators" by their brethren who took pride in Morse code ability. Morse code has always been considered the basic means of communication: something that will get through when nothing else can. However, the most serious type of communication there is — marine distress communication — no longer relies on Morse code, using instead a complex automated system. Morse code continues to be used by amateurs and many commercial services, but it is clearly on the way out and will eventually disappear from active use by any service. Amateurs will continue to use the Morse code for traditional reasons and they may well end up being the only users of this method of communication.

For a large group of people who are expected to comply with rather complex rules, amateur radio operators are a remarkable example of self discipline and government. Operators who disregard the rules soon come to the attention of their brethren, who often point out the errors. Of course, the FCC is the ultimate enforcing body and will act if there is a serious violation of the rules. The FCC in recent years has had to operate with a sharply reduced budget and just doesn't have the manpower to police every detail of amateur operations.

A good example of amateur discipline came with the Pearl Harbor attack on Hawaii in 1941. The day of the attack the amateur frequencies were busy with the usual activity. In fact, amateur stations in Hawaii were on the air at the time the attack occurred and provided the first news to the mainland. These Hawaiian stations were quickly shut down by army patrols in the aftermath of the bombing. On the mainland United States amateur frequencies were busy with their usual activities. By Monday morning all U.S. amateur stations had voluntarily shut down. Only a few stray signals from Cuba and other South American stations could be heard. No one had to tell the amateurs to shut down: some remembered the experiences of World War I, and others knew instinctively that they should not be on the air with a state of war existing.

The FCC issued a formal order on December 8, 1941, suspending all amateur operations. Certain exceptions were initially granted, thus allowing operation by certain stations. These exceptions were canceled by a later order dated January 9, 1942 (appendixes 5 and 6), and all amateur activity was eliminated for the duration of the war. The return to peacetime operations in 1945 was not so orderly. A lot of stations jumped the gun and got back on the air before the official time, most using phony calls to remain anonymous.

In the early period of World War I it was an amateur operator who unmasked the activities of a German-owned coastal station at Sayville, Long Island. The amateur operator listening to the transmissions of the Sayville station discovered that they were sending messages to Nauen, Germany, giving information on Allied shipping for the benefit of enemy submarines. Phonograph recordings were made of the transmissions and with this evidence the government seized the station and placed it under U.S. control.

Amateur operators traditionally obtained their licenses by passing tests administered by government examiners. In 1930, while radio communications were still under the control of the Department of Commerce, there were some 20,000 amateur licensees. The number has grown to over 600,000 today. Eventually the FCC found that it could no longer handle the administrative details of conducting license tests. So amateurs took over the job themselves, using volunteer examiners from their own ranks. The examinations are based on government-approved question lists and there is no suggestion that the process has not been successful, saving the government thousands of dollars each year. The FCC still keeps the permanent records, and issues call letters but is freed from the enormous task of conducting license tests for a steadily growing number of applicants.

Aside from their wartime contributions, amateur radio operators have always had a strong commitment to serve in peacetime emergencies. In 1924 the Midwest was devastated by a series of snow and ice storms that brought down almost all telegraph and telephone wires. At that time most communication lines were in overhead wires and quite vulnerable to storms of this nature. Amateurs quickly recognized the need and went into action to provide communications for railroads, newspapers, medical emergencies, and individuals. All of this was done by Morse code telegraphy, which was the predominant mode at the time. In 1925 the entire nation was absorbed in a tense drama unfolding in Kentucky where a man named Floyd Collins was trapped in Sand Cave. The location was several miles from the nearest telegraph station at Cave City, Kentucky. Two amateur operators set up a temporary station in the cave and provided communication for the rescue effort, as well as transmitting thousands of words of press. The station in the cave was powered by batteries that were donated by the Burgess Battery Company. The two amateur operators, 9BRK and 9CHG, worked for four days without sleep before the rescue effort was finally called off. All efforts to save Floyd Collins had been in vain.

Today's radio amateurs are still following the same tradition. With their repeater stations and radio-equipped cars, amateurs operate networks that rival commercial standards. The work today is done in the high-frequency bands, typically 2 meters or 144 MHz, and using the FM voice mode of operation. The amateurs work in close cooperation with the police, Red Cross, and any other agency that needs auxiliary communication in an emergency. When American Eagle flight 4184 crashed in northern Indiana on Halloween night in 1994, amateurs were ready to help. The crash site was in a remote area where communication lines were limited and immediate service was needed to fill the needs of police, fire, and investigative agencies.

Amateurs are gregarious and tend to seek out others who have the same interest. When most communications tended to be local in nature, operators liked to meet personally just to see what the other fellow looked like. When a group got together the name "hamfest" was coined. Most early hamfests were modest gatherings, usually held at a private home with the host arranging a meal for the guests. These were purely social affairs with maybe a little buying, selling, or trading going on as a result of previous arrangements made over the air. Gradually, as the amateur population grew so did the size of the hamfests. From simple gatherings at a private home they became large affairs held at some public facility. Admission is charged, prizes given, and buying and selling is the main business. Tailgate dealers set up their wares in long rows and the main activity of the attendees is wandering up and down the rows of dealers to see what kinds of bargains can be found.

Haggling over prices is normal and no one is expected to pay the asking price for an item. The action is fast and furious, usually starting as early as 6 A.M. and being all over by noon. Friendships are renewed among the dealers who tend to come back year after year. After the grand prize is awarded most people head home. Perhaps the largest hamfest in the United States is the Dayton Hamvention, held in Dayton, Ohio, in May each year. This is a three-day affair, organized with professional skill. The souvenir program is a 100-page slick paper production. The number of exhibitors and fleamarket dealers at Dayton is so large that only a few people manage to cover the whole area in the three-day period. Attendance is so large that almost all available housing in the Dayton area is sold out. Regular visitors make their room reservations a full year in advance to be sure of their accommodations.

Originally, amateur radio was almost exclusively a male-dominated hobby. Over the years, however, many female operators got on the air and now they are a large percentage of the total number. Unmarried girls are called "YLs" (young ladies) and married operators are called "XYLs." This latter term is sometimes resented by the married ladies, who interpret it as meaning that they are no longer young ladies. As with the Morse telegraph, communication with unseen members of the opposite sex can lead to romances. Many times though when the parties actually meet in person the results are disappointing. There are many husband and wife licensees and this has been a popular aspect of amateur radio in recent years. Modern radios make communication with moving automobiles easy and the married couples enjoy the convenience of instant communication.

In the early years most amateurs were mature adults or at least of high school age. Now, some very young persons, both boys and girls, have taken up the hobby. Usually tutored by a parent who is a licensed operator, some youngsters have qualified for amateur licenses at the tender age of six.

Amateur operators have taken part in many major expeditions to the far corners of the globe. One of the first was Don Mix, W1TS, who acted as radio operator for the Donald MacMillan Arctic expedition in 1923. Operation was on the old 200 meter amateur frequency. MacMillan declared that

4.3. Absorption type wavemeter of 60 years ago. Found at amateur radio flea market (photo by Lewis Coe).

"no polar expedition will attempt to go north again without radio equipment." Amateur operators have taken part in dozens of other expeditions, including both of the Richard Byrd South Pole trips.

The first organized amateur activity grew out of the range limitations of the early type of equipment. To send messages over great distances, the amateurs organized relay routes where messages were sent on from one station to the next. Transcontinental relay of messages was accomplished for the first time in 1921. Out of this early activity came the name of the leading amateur organization: The American Radio Relay League (ARRL). The league is the parent organization of amateur radio and publishes a monthly magazine called *QST* (QST is the international signal for calling all stations) Although the league has no legal status to govern amateur radio, it is the main organized group to present amateur radio problems to the FCC. Amateurs are under no obligation to belong to the ARRL, but a large percentage do, recognizing that the league is the only effective voice they have in dealing with the FCC.

Amateurs still relay messages across the country. Now they do it with sophisticated packet radio links that cover the entire United States. After the long-distance capabilities of high-frequency radio was discovered, amateur communication to almost any place on the globe was possible. Long-distance communications are known as "DX" and form the main interest for many operators. Amateur equipment today is a far cry from the primitive home-built sets of the early days. Most operators use commercially built equipment. The most popular configuration is the transceiver, which combines transmitting and receiving functions in one compact tabletop unit. All modes of operation are provided, the most widely used being single side-band and CW telegraphy. The units have band switching to the various amateur frequency bands and some even have automatic antenna tuners built in. Frequency readout is precise, indicating the exact frequency of transmission and reception.

The new sets are so complex that few operators can build their own anymore. The main focus now is operating skill, although there is still room for creative ability in the design of antennas and other auxiliary station equipment. With over 600,000 licensed stations — all potential buyers of equipment — a large industry exists just to supply the specialized needs of amateur radio. One thing in favor of the former days of home-built equipment was that the operator acquired a pretty good insight into his station. He could fix troubles that occurred and building one's own equipment developed an expertise that could be acquired in no other way. Now, of course, few can troubleshoot their own equipment and must rely on factory service when problems develop.

A large class of nonprofessional radio people exists in the form of the shortwave listeners, known as SWLs. These listeners comb the airwaves for distant broadcasts of all kinds. Some are quite skilled and may eventually become licensed amateurs with transmitting privileges. Another class of operators are the citizens band group, or CBers.

Citizens band radio was conceived after World War II as a licensed, no-code service to make radio communication available to persons who might not need a full commercial license. At first, the frequency band proposed was in the UHF region above 400 MHz. The state of the art at that time did not permit economical manufacture of low-priced equipment for that frequency band. Later, the frequencies in the 27 MHz band were assigned. This permitted the manufacture of low-cost equipment. As late as 1977 operators were required to have licenses and the service grew by leaps and bounds. At one time there was a backlog of 250,000 license applications pending.

The FCC finally could not handle the administrative details of licensing citizens band stations and just abandoned the idea of station licenses for the CB service. The result was that a potentially valuable service became almost useless due to completely irresponsible operating. Citizens band stations were limited by law to 5 watts of power. Once the licensing requirement was lifted, all respect for the law seemed to disappear. Powerful amplifiers were sold to boost the normal 5 watt transmitters to as much as 1,000 watts. Amateur equipment was modified to work on the citizens band and the sky was the limit as far as power was concerned. All sorts of coarse and obscene language was often used by the operators, so the idea that seemed like such a good one just deteriorated to the point where utter chaos existed. Persons who needed short-range communication for some legitimate service were compelled to utilize some of the licensed business service radios as an alternative.

The present legal assignments for CB stations consist of 40 channels between 26.965 MHz and 27.405 MHz. Of these frequencies, Channel 9 at 27.065 MHz and Channel 19 at 27.185 MHz seem to be the most useful. Channel 9 is monitored by some police agencies and is considered an emergency channel. Channel 19 is used by truckers and motorists on the road. Responsible persons make good use of it in exchanging highway information.

• 5 •

Point to Point

After the first and most obvious use of radio was realized in communicating with ships at sea, thoughts turned to other avenues. Looming large in new applications was the thought that radio could compete with ocean cables and landlines for telegraph message handling. This idea was especially attractive since it was realized that radio circuits would be much less costly to establish and maintain. This was particularly true when compared to ocean cable circuits, where the cost of laying the cables and maintaining them was prohibitively expensive. Furthermore, radio offered the possibility of higher transmission speeds than the ocean cables, which at that time were limited to 15 or 20 words per minute. This meant that the profit potential would be higher when a successful radio circuit could be established.

Marconi encountered many difficulties in his first attempts to bridge the Atlantic. The first transmission of the letter "S" in 1901 was only the precursor of a long series of tests before a practical commercial service could be inaugurated. In the discussion of the letter "S" transmission across the Atlantic it was surprising to many observers that no one actually knew what wavelength had been employed. When Sir Ambrose Fleming, designer of the Poldhu transmitting station, was asked about this he replied as follows:

> The wavelength of the electric waves sent out from the Poldhu Marconi station in 1901 was not measured because I did not invent my cymometer or wavemeter until October 1904. The height of the original aerial (1901) was 200 feet but there was a coil of a transformer or "jigger" as we called it, in series with it. My estimate was that the original wavelength must have not been not less than about 3,000 feet (approximately 914 meters) but it was considerably lengthened later on.
>
> I knew at that time that the diffraction or bending of the rays around the earth would be increased by increasing the wavelength and after the first success I was continually urging Marconi to lengthen the wavelength, and that was done when commercial trans-

5.1. United Wireless stock certificate signed by "Christopher Columbus" Wilson who was later sent to prison for fraud.

> mission began. And I remember I designed special cymometers to measure up to 20,000 feet (approximately 6,097 meters) or so. [Cymometer is an obsolete word no longer used.]

Wavelengths used by the Marconi stations got progressively longer as the advantages of ever longer wavelengths were discovered. In 1902 Poldhu was using 1,100 meters, later in the year going to 1,650 meters. By 1904 Poldhu and Glace Bay were on 3,660 meters with Poldhu going to 4,250 meters later in that year. Both stations later used 7,500 and 8,000 meters. In 1907 the Clifden station was using 6,666 meters. Marconi received the historic tuning patent, Number 7777, in 1900. For the first time this enabled tuning the receivers to discreet wavelengths and made it possible for more than one wireless station to operate in a local area at the same time.

Unfortunately, many of the early wireless promoters were more interested in selling stock and making money than they were in advancing the radio art. Wireless was the wonder of the age and the eager public required little persuasion to invest money. One of Lee De Forest's early ventures was the United Wireless Telegraph Company (see photo 5.1). De Forest himself was sincere in his desire to provide good communications by the new medium. His associates, however, were more interested in the profit potential of the enterprise. In the end, De Forest inherited the ill will and liabilities

5.2. Original 200 kilowatt Alexanderson Alternator still preserved in working order at Radio Station SAQ, Grimeton, Sweden (photo courtesy Swedish Telcom).

of the company while his associates made off with all that was profitable. One of these men, whose name appears on many of United's stock certificates, "Christopher Columbus" Wilson, was finally brought to account and ended up in federal prison for his part in the stock-selling fraud.

Prior to World War I the formula for bridging long distances by radio was low frequency, high power, and a big antenna. Pushing all of these factors to the maximum would usually result in a practical circuit. Spark gap transmitters had just about reached the limit of power in the early 1900s. Something better was needed, and this appeared after 1909 when Federal Telegraph brought the first arc transmitter to the United States from Denmark and started building ever larger units. When a 30 kw Federal arc outperformed the navy's 100 kw spark transmitter, it led the way to more efficient operations. The arc generated for the first time a continuous wave that was much more effective at spanning distance than the broad wave emitted by even the best of the spark transmitters. Ever more powerful arcs were built, culminating with the 1,000 kw units built in France in 1918.

The arc soon had a competitor for the generation of continuous-wave energy in the form of the high-frequency alternator. The alternator transmitter, which in simple terms was a high-frequency alternating current generator coupled to a radiating antenna, was the brainchild of Reginald

Fessenden. Fessenden was convinced that his idea would work and commissioned the General Electric Company to build an alternator for him. General Electric assigned the project to a young Swedish engineer, Ernst Alexanderson. A successful alternator was built and delivered to Fessenden and used in many of his early experiments.

With the experience gained in the Fessenden project, Alexanderson went on to solve the many problems associated with building practical machines. Eventually, he arrived at a design that made the 200 kw alternator a commercial item that could be manufactured and sold with every confidence that it would work. Alexanderson (1878–1975), was born in Sweden and received a classical education in electrical engineering in Stockholm and Berlin. Arriving in the United States in 1902, he found work with General Electric's test department. Many other young Swedes did the same thing, for the test department at GE was thought to be the ideal place for a young engineer to start his career. Beginning in the test department at the magnificent salary of 17.5 cents per hour, Alexanderson after only five months had advanced to the engineering department at the princely salary of $19 per week. Aside from his success with the alternator project, Alexanderson made a name for himself in the design of a wide variety of electrical equipment. In his lifetime he had accumulated a total of 344 patents. The last one, a motor control device was issued in 1973, two years before his death.

Both Fessenden and Alexanderson had reached the correct conclusion that a radio or hertzian wave is alternating current electricity, which is the same, except for frequency, as the 60 Hz current used to light lamps and run motors. Thus, they reasoned, all that was needed to transmit radio waves was a high-frequency generator, capable of generating frequencies that would radiate in space. This was a simplistic approach in principle, yet it was enormously complicated in practical application. The frequency of an alternator is determined by the number of poles in the magnetic field and the speed of the rotor. To generate frequencies higher than 10 kHz required many poles and a high-speed rotor and this presented great problems when any considerable amount of power was involved.

The final design of the Alexanderson alternator involved a solid steel rotor 64 inches in diameter with teeth milled into the circumference running within 0.035 inch of the stationary field winding, having many poles. Many problems had to be solved in arriving at a practical design that could be put into commercial production. Bearings and windings had to be cooled to dissipate heat, and speed regulation of the rotor had to be exact to maintain the emitted frequency at a constant value. Final design of the speed regulation system gave an accuracy of 0.1 percent. In addition, keying of the output for radio telegraphy had to be accomplished. This was done by the so-called magnetic amplifier. The magnetic amplifier was a static device with no moving parts. The antenna output of the alternator was passed through the one winding of the magnetic amplifier. Then, by applying direct current bias to another winding of the amplifier, the output could be keyed in Morse code.

Alternators were huge machines. Even the first 50 kw alternator weighed 22 tons and required a 10-horse team to transport it from the railhead to the New Brunswick, New Jersey, station where it was installed. Later, the alternator was scaled up to 200 kw and these machines weighed about 30 tons. Mounted on massive cast-iron bases, the machines resembled large motor generator sets as used in the electric power industry. Installation of one, with all of the auxiliary apparatus required, was a job requiring several months. Nevertheless, the alternator was a reliable device, whose performance could be counted on.

They were sold all over the world and formed the basis for the original RCA worldwide communications system. Installed at Rocky Point, New York, they remained in service until World War II. The antennas at Rocky Point were 10 wire flat-top affairs 1,250 feet long on 410 feet high steel towers. The last of these towers was dynamited in 1977 and in 1978 RCA announced the gift of 7,100 acres of land to the New York State Department of Environmental Conservation. For many years the old low-frequency alternator transmitters at Rocky Point had only been used as a backup during poor propagation conditions on the normal shortwave channels. Even with the general move to shortwave communication, the alternators continued to fill special needs.

In 1942 an alternator at Tuckerton, New Jersey, operating on 15.8 kHz was used for communication with naval vessels. In 1944 the alternator in Hawaii was started up and continued in operation until 1957, performing valuable service for communication with submarines. The U.S. Air Force utilized the alternator at Marion, Massachusetts, for communicating with air bases in Greenland and Iceland from 1949 to 1961. The low-frequency signals generated by the alternators tended to be more reliable than shortwaves in the polar regions and in communicating with submerged submarines.

Two hundred kw is a lot of power, matched by few present-day transmitters, where 50 kw is considered a high-power station. When the 200 kw transmitter was in operation at New Brunswick, New Jersey, during World War I, the station was under navy control. The sentries patrolling the grounds used to complain that the intense radio frequency field in the immediate vicinity created a corona discharge from the bayonets on their rifles. Also, it was necessary to ground vehicles and gasoline hose nozzles during refueling as any metal object created a spark discharge.

5.3. Antenna system for Alexanderson Alternator at SAQ, Grimeton, Sweden (photo courtesy Swedish Telecom).

When two of the 200 kw units were sold to Poland, unique problems were encountered in the installation. The Poles would not settle for just any building to house their new transmitter. The buildings had to be constructed with traditional architecture, "to reflect the true architectural feeling of Poland." When finally completed, these two units served well. After Germany overran Poland during World War II, the station was used to communicate with German submarines. The station was finally destroyed by the Germans to prevent it from falling into Russian hands in the closing phases of the war.

Alternators installed in Sweden also had a long life. The Swedish station was located at Grimeton, near Varberg. One of the two units was scrapped in 1960 but the other one was still operable in 1986 and went on the air to send a commemorative message. SAQ, the Swedish station, transmitted on 17.2 kHz (photos 5.2, 5.3). The alternator had a 976 pole stator and the rotor turned at 2,115 rpm. The commemorative message quoted David Sarnoff, president of RCA as saying, "When the history of RCA is written, it must begin with Alexanderson and his alternator, for without him there would be no RCA today." In a radio speech during World War II, Alexanderson characterized the Swedish alternator as the "old war horse, because it always gets the message through."

The remaining alternator at Grimeton may be the last of its kind. The old machine is no longer used but has been preserved in operating condition along with its associated antenna system. This is important to note because the antennas used with the alternators were unique and were essential to the proper operation of the overall system. Most of the other alternators have been scrapped and with their 30 ton bulk they had considerable scrap value. Apparently, General Electric did not even preserve the engineering drawings used to build the alternators once they stopped selling them. The Swedish authorities deserve a great deal of credit for preserving a significant portion of communications history.

The worldwide communication system utilizing the high-power arc and alternator transmitters continued to function until the early 1920s. Then exciting new discoveries about the propagation of short wavelength signals began to challenge the old theories of using long waves and high power. Amateur radio operators being confined to wavelengths below 200 meters had no choice but to use them. They began to achieve spectacular distances using low power and the wavelengths below 200 meters. This amateur work was not unnoticed by the commercial companies, notably Marconi in England. It was found that high-frequency signals around 30 meters in wavelength were reflected from the ionosphere and came back to earth thousands of miles away. By the proper choice of wavelength, and using highly directive antennas, it was possible to achieve worldwide communication with a fraction of the power used before.

In 1924 Marconi announced their new "beam system," and RCA in America and other companies throughout the world followed the Marconi lead. A further advantage of the shortwave system was that it permitted higher signaling speeds due to generally stronger signals at the receiver and the absence of atmospheric interference. The British Post Office used their high-speed Wheatstone equipment on the new radio links and often ran at speeds of 200 words per minute. This increased the profitability of the radio circuits immensely as the ocean cables were still running at slower speeds.

Point-to-point services, also known as the fixed services, were at first confined to international circuits where they offered many advantages over ocean cables. In the United States radio soon attracted attention as a possible alternative to the land telegraph lines. In 1911 the Federal Telegraph Company, which had acquired the rights to use the Poulsen arc from Denmark, decided to establish a domestic radio telegraph network to compete with the land telegraph. Stations using the arc transmitters on frequencies below 100 kHz were established in Chicago, El Paso, Fort Worth, Kansas City, Los Angeles, Portland, San Diego, San Francisco, and Seattle.

These stations were surprisingly modern for their time. Transmission speeds up to 80 words per minute were possible. High-speed receiving was accomplished by another Poulsen invention, the magnetic wire recorder. Messages could be recorded at high speed and then the playback slowed down for copying by the operator. These circuits worked pretty well under favorable nighttime conditions, but performance was marginal during daylight hours. The service to the inland points was finally discontinued by the time of World War I. The Pacific coast network, with shorter distances and more uniform weather conditions, was kept in operation right up to the time of World War II, when all domestic radio operations were shut down. Still operating on the original low-frequency channels, this arc network was the last of its kind. The radio service operated by Federal Telegraph and later Mackay Radio competed with the landline telegraph by offering "15 words for the price of 10."

Henry Ford, always innovative, especially when it came to cutting costs and improving efficiency, was quick to take advantage of radio communication. In 1920 he started experimenting with radio communication as an alternative to wire links between several of his plants. Stations were established in Dearborn, Michigan, KDEN; Springfield, Ohio, WNA; Flat Rock, Michigan, WFD; and Northville, Michigan, KDEP. This was essentially a point-to-point radio telegraph network, using manual sending and receiving of messages in Morse code. The radio net saved Ford thousands of dollars in telegraph and telephone charges on routine messages between plants. At first radiotelephony was tried, but it was found that executives tended to be long-winded when communicating by voice, and so thereafter the operation was exclusively telegraphic. The radio net operated on wavelengths between 465 and 520 meters in what would later become the broadcast band. The Ford stations were actually licensed for broadcasting, even though this privilege was rarely used. One of the few times that broadcasting was used was when Edsel Ford went on the air to announce a cut in tractor production.

There was no other attempt to compete with the landline services until 1933 when Mackay Radio and RCA established domestic networks using the same high-frequency channels that were used for international communication. The equipment and methods of both companies also followed the same designs that had proved reliable in international service. Stations were established in Chicago, Los Angeles, New Orleans, New York, Portland, San Francisco, Seattle, and Washington, D.C. Other points were in the planning stage when World War II brought an end to operations.

The Mackay Radio stations in northern Indiana formed the connection with Chicago for the point-to-point network. The transmitter at St. John, Indiana, was located on a 90 acre tract of marginal farmland that the company acquired for a bargain price during those Depression days of 1933 (photos 5.4, 5.5). At 67 Broad Street in New York an engineer pored over the plot plan and made a mark in the exact geometric center of the plot to indicate the site of the transmitter building (photos 5.4, 5.5). This was the location that permitted a good distribution of the poles and transmission lines that fed the various high-frequency antennas. Unfortunately, the site for the building was also the lowest point on the property and almost at the edge of a rather large lake that existed. At certain seasons the lake level came up and it was necessary to construct a long walkway on posts to provide entrance to the building.

Location over a swampy area is considered ideal for long-wave transmitting stations that benefit from good ground conductivity. Mackay's marine coastal station, WSL, at Amagansett, New York, was located on a saltwater marsh and required a long causeway for access. Transmitting stations for the high-frequency channels as used at St. John do not depend primarily on ground conductivity. After the station at St. John was abandoned during World War II the lake level increased so much that today the foundation of the old building is actually under water the year round. The increased lake level is probably due to extensive building in the area, which increased the runoff of rain water and it has all collected in the lake.

The companion receiving station for the St. John transmitter was located on a 120 acre site near the town of Merrillville, Indiana. It was about 10 miles from the St. John transmitter. This was normal practice in locating such stations. It permitted full duplex operation with no interference from the local transmitters. The Merrillville site was picked because it was then a pretty remote place with only a dirt country road for access. This was considered necessary to avoid interference from automobile ignition systems, which were not as well designed to reduce spark plug interference then as they are now.

As luck would have it, after about five years of operation at the Merrillville site a highway relocation project got underway in this part of Indiana. The former country road became a four-lane state highway. Automobile ignition interference did not prove to be a problem and the station continued in successful operation until all domestic radio services were closed down in 1942. The Merrillville station took part in the stratosphere balloon experiments of the 1930s. Launched from the "stratobowl" near Rapids City, South Dakota, the balloon carried high-frequency transmitters, and stations all over the world listened for the signals. The object was to determine if radio waves would penetrate outer space, an important consideration for later space programs. Merrillville station is now the location of a busy shopping mall and it is hard to imagine it as a remote farm field where serious radio work was being done.

Mackay Radio used Postal Telegraph for local pickup and delivery of messages and RCA had a similar arrangement with Western Union. The

Top: 5.4. Mackay Radio transmitting station near St. John, Indiana. Handled telegraph traffic between Chicago, New York and San Francisco; *bottom:* 5.5. Interior of Mackay Radio transmitting station, showing 10 kw transmitter used for Chicago–San Francisco traffic (both photos by Lewis Coe).

radio circuits attracted a
large volume of traffic and
were quite reliable. The
needs of the business community had outgrown the
services offered by the
landline companies. Large
users had direct connec-
tions to the radio operating
rooms and thus achieved
much faster delivery time.

World War II brought
an end to all domestic
radio operations. Signals
from the domestic network
could be heard worldwide
and it was not feasible to
apply censorship to the
domestic traffic as was
done with international
traffic. The concern was
that the enemy would
monitor the domestic mes-
sages and gain useful information. The domestic net-
works were never resumed
after the war. The merger

5.6. Mackay Radio 50 kilowatt shortwave transmitter installed at Algiers, North Africa, to initiate postwar radio service to New York (photo by
Lewis Coe).

of Postal Telegraph and Western Union had effectively ended the possibility
of competition for domestic telegraph traffic. Also, the high-frequency channels used by the domestic services were needed for a growing international
service. Ironically, satellite technology has now resulted in an actual decrease
of the need for the high-frequency channels that were so heavily occupied
after the war. Although World War II marked the end of domestic radiotelegraph service, be it longwave arc or shortwave vacuum tube transmitters,
some form of radio has emerged as the final domestic carrier.

Microwave relay routes and satellite links now carry most of the communications that are not routed over coaxial or fiber-optic cable. In countries where all communication was government controlled there was little
use of radio to compete with landlines. Before Alaska became a state the territory had a telegraph system operated by the Army Signal Corps. Soon after
the original Morse lines were established, experiments started with wireless.
It was soon found that in most cases the overall performance of the wireless

links was superior to the landlines. The landlines were difficult to keep in working order under the harsh Alaskan weather conditions. It was common practice to have shelter cabins along the telegraph lines. The cabins were stocked with wire, insulators, and a quantity of alcohol to be used for starting fires. The regulations were very strict about using the alcohol for other than its intended purpose! Billy Mitchell, the original builder of the Alaskan telegraph system, later became famous for his struggle to prove the value of air power in warfare.

The very first transmissions of voice signals by

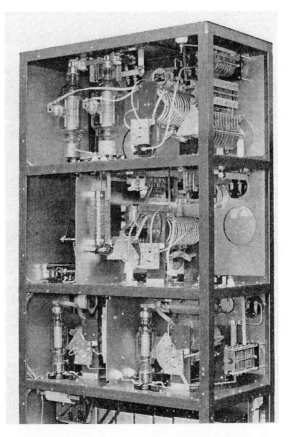

5.7. Interior of 1 kw. shortwave transmitter manufactured by Federal Telegraph Co., 1933 (photo by Lewis Coe).

radio attracted the interest of the telephone company. Any method of sending voice signals by methods other than the costly wire lines offered tremendous potential. In 1906 Fessenden had succeeded in making voice transmissions with a low-power alternator. Hammond Hayes of the telephone company, on the basis of a report by Edwin Colpitts (see biographies below), made a report to President Fish of the Bell System as follows: "I feel that there is such a reasonable probability of wireless telegraphy and telephony being of commercial value to our company that I would advise taking steps to associate ourselves with Mr. Fessenden if some satisfactory arrangement can be made."

Negotiations were started with Fessenden and were close to a final agreement when the financial panic of 1907 hit the country. This brought many changes in the Bell management, including a relocation of the head-quarters to New York City. All expenditures were being scrutinized very closely and it was finally decided not to buy the Fessenden patents. Thomas Lockwood, the Bell patent lawyer summarized the reasons for the decision as follows:

> If an individual or a corporation is desirous of becoming interested in wireless telephony for the sake of keeping in touch with progress in electrical transmission work, based on recent scientific research, this would seem to be an excellent opportunity, but for a telephone company, the possibility of substituting a wireless system for a system of toll lines is the most attractive feature of the proposition, and I have a strong conviction that this feature cannot and will not reach any practical realization within the term of years yet remaining to Fessenden's fundamental patents.

This was a remarkably accurate assessment made by Lockwood, as was proven by subsequent events. It would be many years before radio technology reached the stage where it would be useful to the telephone company. Except for the Catalina Island link and long-haul international circuits, the telephone company made little use of radio until microwave research began in the early 1930s. Then it began to appear that there was a good possibility of using radio waves to supplement the costly wire lines. Research was necessarily postponed due to the emergency of World War II. In April 1944 Bell Laboratories announced its plans as follows:

> Plans for the trial of a new type of intercity communications facility were announced on March 16 by the American Telephone and Telegraph Company. The work will take two years to complete and will cost more than $2,000,000. It will supplement present commercial long distance telephone facilities and provide network facilities for the transmission of television programs between New York, Boston and intermediate points.
>
> Application is being made to the Federal Communications Commission for approval to begin the project, which is expected to proceed as rapidly as the war situation permits. At present engineers of these Laboratories essential to technical phases of the undertaking are engaged in war work.
>
> The new system will be operated by radio relays of a type which was under development by the Laboratories prior to the war. This system applies to communication by radio many of the techniques which have played an important part in the development of long distance wire telephone circuits. Directed radio beams at ultra-high

frequencies will operate simultaneously in both directions and these will be relayed at stations spaced at an average of about thirty miles throughout the route. It is hoped that, ultimately, each radio beam will carry a large number of communications channels.

The New York–Boston circuit went into operation on November 13, 1947. It was followed by New York–Chicago and eventually the transcontinental links came into service. Microwave radio relay systems opened new horizons in communication (photo 5.8). Capacity of the systems was expanded to carry 21,600 telephone channels. The multitude of circuits now available made nationwide direct dialing possible in 1951 and eliminated the need for the old Morse order wire circuits that were standard in the days of open wire.

5.8. One of the original concrete microwave towers on AT&T's New York to Chicago circuit (photo by Lewis Coe).

Microwave techniques have proved so useful and flexible that they have been adopted by almost all long-distance telephone carriers, the railroads, pipelines, the FAA, and many other agencies who need dependable point-to-point communication. The old point-to-point services using low- and high-frequency bands have disappeared in the United States. Open wire lines have virtually disappeared except along some railroads that still retain them. Even Western Union had adopted microwave radio relay to replace its open wire lines before its final demise in 1989.

Probably few persons outside of the industry realize the huge amount of telegraph traffic that passes between countries of the world. Especially heavy is the traffic between the United States and Europe. Normally heavy in peacetime conditions, the traffic increased to an extremely high level during World War II. The ocean cables of that era had limited capacity and the balance of the traffic was handled by radio. All of the major communication companies, Mackay Radio, Press Wireless, and RCA had multichannel, high-speed radio telegraph circuits in operation to Moscow and London. The circuits operated 24 hours a day at speeds approaching 200 words per minute when conditions permitted. These were two-way circuits, and there was just as much traffic moving from East to West as there was outgoing from the United States.

Aside from their regular function of providing radiotelegraph services to existing locations, all the U.S. radio companies were active in providing special services during World War II. Mobile units were sent into France and provided instantaneous communication of press dispatches to New York. As soon as the city of Paris was liberated, Mackay Radio established a station there and opened a regular circuit to New York. The same was done in North Africa, where a complete station was shipped in by Mackay Radio and installed on the premises of the local Post and Telegraph administration at Algiers. When the Italians pulled out of Ethiopia, they completely destroyed the radio station at Addis Ababa. In 1945 a Mackay Radio engineer arrived in Addis Ababa and started the process of rebuilding the station. Some of the remnants of the transmitter were found on the junk pile. Eventually, a direct circuit was established between Addis Ababa and New York. All of these activities helped to restore the worldwide communications system that had been ravaged by war (photos 5.6, 5.7).

Ever since communication channels started operating in the high-frequency portion of the spectrum, the National Bureau of Standards was active in investigating propagation characteristics of the frequencies involved. The radio communications companies cooperated in this work by regularly forwarding transcripts of their daily circuit logs to the bureau. These logs recorded actual circuit conditions on the various international channels. This information enabled the bureau to check its theoretical predictions against actual circuit conditions.

Up until the time of World War II, most radio telegraph transmitters used make and break keying, the original method used on all wireless transmitters. When the key was closed a signal was transmitted, when it was open nothing was heard. This method of keying, still used in many applications, began to exhibit limitations when high-speed keying was involved. During the key open condition, the receivers were vulnerable to random noise and atmospheric disturbances. A new method of keying was developed, called frequency shift. With the new keying, the key was never opened. Instead, the transmitting frequency was moved a controlled amount to transmit the dot and dash signals. This enabled a better design of the receiving equipment and greatly increased the reliability of reception.

Analagous to FM radio in the ability to operate under conditions of heavy noise and static, frequency shift keying became the preferred method for high-speed radiotelegraphy. The method was so reliable that after the war it was used to provide press dispatch service for small newspapers in Central and South America. The newspapers were provided with a receiving terminal that was tuned to the transmitter in the United States. These were receiving terminals only and the reliability was such that the teleprinters in the newspaper offices seldom failed to deliver the daily quota of news dispatches. The frequency shift method was, in fact, what made possible the operation of teleprinters directly from radio signals. The old on-off keying would operate a teleprinter when conditions were optimum but caused many errors when noise and static entered the receiver. Originally, the transmitting tape for radio telegraph circuits was punched in Morse code. When printers came into operation, the transmitting tape was punched in either five-element Baudot or ASCII code.

High-frequency radio was the first carrier for overseas radiotelephone circuits. Starting in 1956, however, telephone cables with underwater repeaters began to go into service. Now a multiplicity of telephone cables, including the fiber-optic cables, has just about ended the days of high-frequency radio for point-to-point telephone circuits. The satellite facilities augment the cables and offer the means of reaching the most remote spots in the world. The telephone company closed its station at Lawrenceville, New Jersey — long a key site in the radio network — in 1976. Radiotelegraph circuits have also just about disappeared from the HF bands. At one time they were active in linking all the world capitals. Now the communication companies find it is more cost effective to lease the necessary facilities on a satellite or fiber-optic cable than to maintain elaborate ground radio stations. All of the old point-to-point stations on Long Island, Rocky Point, Riverhead, Brentwood, and Southampton have long since been abandoned.

Once the beam system of shortwave communication had been established, shortwave radiotelegraph circuits were set up to all the major cities of the world. These shortwave facilities consisted of separate transmitting and receiving stations, usually separated by distances of 10 to 20 miles. This permitted full duplex operation of a multiplicity of transmitters and receivers. A typical receiving station might have 25 or more circuits to various foreign points. The receivers were usually arranged in groups of three in what was known as the diversity system of reception. The diversity system employed a separate antenna for each of the three receivers in the group. The three antennas were spaced far enough apart so that the arriving signal did not hit each one at the same instant. By combining the outputs of the three receivers, the normal effects of fading could be minimized.

The receiver outputs were sent by wire line or microwave link to the operating center that was normally located in the central part of the city involved. There the signals were recorded by a siphon recorder on paper tape, which was then sight-read by the operator. This was essentially the same method long used on ocean cables, except that the speed was much higher. At high speeds the receiving tape or "slip" could be split up among two or more operators so that there was no delay in transcribing the Morse code signals.

At the remote receiving station there might be three or more operators on duty during busy periods of the day. The job of these operators was to constantly monitor the incoming signals and make any needed adjustments in the receiver tuning. They also made switching changes to other frequencies as might be required by propagation conditions. The receiving station operators got their instructions by Morse telegraph from the city operating room. The telegraph instruments could be heard all over the room. Sending keys were placed at convenient locations along the rows of receivers. Thus an operator could respond to a call wherever he or she happened to be and did not have to go to a central point to answer. These Morse circuits were eventually replaced by teleprinters of telephones, but most of the old-timers thought the Morse system was ideally suited to the operation and easier to use. During the heyday of radio telegraph operation, most of each company's personnel were quite proficient in Morse. Often the senior executives were persons who had come up through the ranks and for them Morse was a second language. It was not uncommon to find telegraph instruments on polished desks in the executive offices of the communications companies.

Transmitting stations involved a much larger installation physically than the receivers. The necessary equipment took up much more room and involved a great deal of auxiliary equipment. The individual transmitter cabinets — which might be about as large as the average kitchen — were arranged in rows and the controls routed to a central panel that in turn connected to the city operating center. The duty of the transmitting station operators was to periodically check each unit to make sure it was operating correctly and was within tolerance of the assigned frequency channel. The operators also shut down and started different transmitters and shifted frequency channels in response to instructions received from the city office. The output of each transmitter was connected to a directional antenna oriented to give the maximum signal in the distant receiver. The sending signal was keyed in Morse code, generated by a punched paper tape prepared on a punching machine with a typewriter-style keyboard. The punched tape was run through a transmitting head to send the signals to the remote radio transmitter. The tape could be run at any desired speed up to 200 words per minute or so as conditions permitted.

This was the basic shortwave radiotelegraph service as pioneered by Marconi and then adopted by companies all over the world. It was a very flexible system and since it used Morse code it could be slowed down to manual speed when conditions were too poor to use high-speed operation.

Writing in *Communication and Electronics* in November 1952, Haraden Pratt speculated on the possibility of using the newly developed microwave technology for international communication. The method was already in use for transcontinental telephony and was proving very successful. Pratt wondered if the same technique could not be used on the "land bridge" connecting North America with Asia. This was the route that was to carry the Western Union landline connecting North America with Asia. Construction had already started on this line, only to be abandoned after the successful laying of the first Atlantic telegraph cable in 1866. One can only wonder, assuming that this 1866 line had been completed, as to just how reliable it would have been in operation. The severe weather conditions over much of the route and the difficulties of transportation in that era would seem to preclude very reliable performance. Pratt wrote at a time when the present satellite technology and fiber-optic cables were far in the future. Apparently, there was no further consideration of an overland route. It would have been a difficult project at best, but probably would have had a better chance of reliable operation than the 1866 wire-line project.

•6•

Potpourri

A host of services operate under a classification that FCC calls low-power devices. Low-power devices operate with full authority of the FCC but they are sharply limited as to how much power they can radiate and they are assigned to definite frequency bands. No station or operator license is required for this class of equipment and in many cases it fills the bill for communication with the minimum of complications. All that is required is that the user purchase the equipment from a manufacturer who has complied with the FCC specifications.

One of the first such devices to become widely used was the ubiquitous garage door opener. Few persons having a motorized garage door would want to be without one now, yet they were quite a novelty when first introduced. The first garage door openers employed a small tube-type transmitter operating on a radio frequency channel around 27 MHz. When the transmitter was activated, the radio wave triggered a tube that controlled the door opening motor. Unlike today's handheld transmitters, the early ones required permanent installation in the car's engine compartment with a dashboard-mounted pushbutton to activate the door-opening mechanism.

These first openers were subject to false operation from lightning disturbances and often a single transmitter unit would activate the neighbor's door as well. Modern openers, operating around 300 MHz, are more sophisticated in design and are encoded so that the receiver only responds to the owner's individual signal. In addition to the door openers, remote-control devices are available to turn on interior house lights or other functions. These remote units also use radio frequencies around 300 MHz.

The so-called baby monitors are another low-power radio device that has come into widespread use. These monitors consist of a low-power 49 MHz FM radio transmitter with a sensitive microphone and a mating receiver tuned to the transmitter frequency. Like other low-power devices, the range of baby monitor transmitters is limited, yet it can vary widely under certain conditions. Often these baby monitor signals can be heard up and down a city block. This has led to some rather impromptu broadcasts. A young couple retire to their bedroom after junior is safely asleep. The monitor is left on, picking up every sound in the room. The listening neighbor may then hear a surprisingly frank broadcast from the bedroom!

Fast food restaurants make extensive use of low-power radio sets for communication between the drive-in order station and the clerks who fill the orders. This is how they are able to have the order ready when your car is driven to the pickup window. A car arriving at the outdoor order station activates a signal that is heard inside the building. When a customer gives his order it is heard by the people who wear headsets and they can assemble the order by the time the customer arrives at the pickup window. Some of these radios operate in the 154 Hz band of frequencies, while others may use lower frequencies in the vicinity of 30 MHz. Although these radios are technically low-power, limited-range devices, they often have surprising range. In one small Midwestern city a good scanner can monitor the signals up to one mile away. Surprisingly frank conversations sometimes occur between the clerks wearing headsets. They can gossip with each other and are not heard by the drive-in customer.

Wireless microphones are another of the low-power devices that have been useful in the entertainment industry. Having a microphone not hampered by a connecting cord is a big advantage. Wireless microphones intended for stage use employ high-quality receivers to provide good reproduction of music. The wireless microphones have also become a favorite tool of auctioneers. The auctioneer can move about the sale grounds and have his voice carried by a powerful loudspeaker. Here again, for low-power devices, the units often have surprising range. At an auction a person with a scanner can sit in his car and follow the progress of the sale. How does he know where to listen? Most of the receiving units have the operating frequency (usually around 169 MHz) stamped on the nameplate in a visible location. By jotting down these figures it is a simple matter to punch in the right frequency on the scanner.

The old-style telephones were sometimes tapped by substituting a tiny FM radio transmitter for the regular transmitter button in the telephone. This kind of tap cannot be used much anymore because, since after deregulation, telephones vary so much in construction. Cordless telephones have become very popular but, unfortunately, they have some disadvantages. Cordless phones employ a small FM transmitter operating in the 47 MHz range and a mating receiver in the base and handset units. These are very low-power devices and have a limited range. Radio waves however, do not always behave according to set rules. The transmitters used in the cordless equipment are intended to be just powerful enough to cover the average home. There must be some margin of excess power to ensure adequate performance, and therefore the range of these units is often much more than expected. Driving through a residential area with a scanner can often reveal dozens of cordless conversations that are audible at least a block away from the home using such a phone. The public is being made increasingly aware of this defect and warned that confidential matters should not be discussed on cordless phones.

The newer cordless models employ sophisticated circuitry operating around 900 MHz, which makes monitoring by unauthorized listeners almost impossible. The newer units are at least double the price of the previous designs and it will be a long time before the older models are all taken out of service. Until that happens, caution is the word when conversing on the cordless phones. Wireless telephone jacks allow the distribution of telephone circuits over the ordinary house wiring. The transmitter unit is plugged into an electrical outlet and the incoming telephone line plugged into it. Then receiver units can be plugged into electrical outlets anywhere in the home to provide a telephone extension line without actually running wires. These units actually use a low-power FM transmitter with a companion receiver. Plugging them into an electrical outlet provides the operating power and the household electrical system acts as a coupling antenna for the radio waves.

Radio communication sets employing headset receivers and boom mikes operate in the low-power, no-license category on frequencies in the 49 MHz range and are useful for personal communication. Like the other low-power devices, these units are limited to short distances, usually not more than a mile. They also occasionally cover much longer ranges than would be normally expected.

Low-power equipment is also used for the radio control of model airplanes, boats, and cars. In flying model aircraft some spectacular maneuvers can be performed by a skilled operator. The army flies radio-controlled aircraft for more serious purposes. The radio-controlled drone planes are used for aerial target practice and for flying cameras into enemy territory for observation purposes. Even the large companies use radio control for their machinery. The Caterpillar Company, certainly not a name associated with toys or lightweight items, has long used radio control for large cranes operating in its facilities. At the company's Mossville, Illinois, plant huge overhead bridge cranes of 10 and 20 ton capacity with an 80 feet span use radio control. The cranes are used to lift diesel engines and move them into the test cells. These cranes were refitted in 1990 with stepless variable speed–drive radio-operated controls.

Military electronic detectors for finding land mines use various radio frequencies to accomplish the detection of buried objects. The same holds true for the metal detectors used by amateur treasure hunters. The army's

Detector Set AN/PRS-1 was widely used during World War II. It used radio frequencies in the range of 280–330 MHz and would detect objects as much as five inches below the surface of the ground. The whole outfit was packed in a carrying case and weighed 65 pounds. All of the metal detectors, whether military or civilian, usually operate on the principle that a buried object will cause a variation in the radiated field from the instrument. This variation can be indicated by a change in audible tone heard in headphones or by a dip in the needle of the indicating instrument.

Other low-power radio services that are now seeing widespread use are the highway information broadcasts. These are low-power, limited-range transmitters operating in the AM broadcast band, usually at the low- or high-frequency end where there are no active broadcast stations. These stations differ from the other low-power services in that they must have an FCC license. This is due to the operation in the standard broadcast band where improper operation could interfere with regular broadcasting. These transmitters are located at strategic points on main highways and carry repetitive tape broadcasts giving highway information bulletins. Their presence is announced by highway signs giving the operating frequency.

Low-powered radio transmitters attached to weather balloons automatically transmit high-altitude weather data to ground receivers. Called radiosondes, they eventually come back to earth and at one time they could be taken to any post office by the finder for postage-paid return to the Weather Bureau. Low-powered transmitters are often used by wildlife biologists to track the movements of wild animals. The transmitters are capable of operating for a considerable time on the self-contained batteries and put out a distinctive signal that can be heard for some distance. Typically, the tracking is done from small aircraft and the receivers are equipped with directive antennas. In order to attach the radio collar the animals are shot with a tranquilizer dart. At the same time an examination of the animal can be made and essential data recorded. Low-powered radios find many uses. They are used by internal security forces at shopping malls and other large buildings and industrial plants. One specialized use that is becoming more popular is in auto racing, where the drivers now routinely keep in touch with their pit crews.

Today's farms are typically operated by one or two people and may cover 1,000 acres or more. Covering this much territory with a limited number of people requires good communication between units in the fields. For this reason, farmers have enthusiastically adopted radio for their operations. Farm radios are typically FM transceivers operating around 150 MHz. They are not classified as low-power devices and require an FCC license to operate. These licenses are easy to get and are normally issued on a routine basis to purchasers of type-approved equipment.

Radio frequency energy is used in many ways aside from communication. It had been discovered as early as 1890 that high-frequency energy was capable of heating human tissue without much discomfort to the patient. Diathermy, as it is called, became a popular treatment used by many physicians in the 1930s. The machines in use at that time consisted of a simple high-frequency oscillator. The oscillator tube ran at fairly high-power levels and was self-excited so that the frequency was not very stable. The radio frequency energy was transferred to the patient by flexible connecting cables with metal plates that were applied to the patient's body. Using this apparatus it was possible to apply localized heat, which was thought to be beneficial. About this time, commercial shortwave point-to-point radio receiving stations started experiencing random interference to their radio telegraph circuits. A strong signal would appear, then move to another frequency. Finally, the interference was traced to diathermy machines. These unstable oscillators working around 13 MHz could interfere with radio communications throughout the United States under certain conditions. Whenever the flexible cables leading to the patient moved, the frequency was changed causing interference to another telegraph channel. The FCC was forced to issue regulations governing the design of diathermy machines to ensure frequency stability and designated frequencies were specified.

In 1945 the FCC assigned the following frequencies for medical diathermy use: 40.98 MHz, 27.32 MHz, and 13.66 MHz. Frequencies in this range were termed short wave diathermy, as distinguished from the earlier use of lower frequencies in the range of 500–3,000 kHz. With the development of radar came the discovery that energy in the microwave region was more efficient for medical purposes. This led the FCC to assign a microwave channel of 2,450 MHz for medical use.

The popular microwave ovens take advantage of the poor dielectric properties of food. When microwaves are applied to a poor dielectric, heat is generated. The ovens use a microwave oscillator, operating on a frequency of 2,450 MHz and are well shielded to confine the energy to the oven enclosure. Originally, the FCC had allocated frequencies of 915 MHz, 2,450 MHz, and 5,500 MHz for microwave ovens. Eventually, the 2,450 MHz became the standard frequency and is shared with medical equipment. Microwave ovens incorporate a powerful source of microwave energy that is potentially dangerous. For this reason construction of the ovens is subject to careful regulation to ensure that there is a minimum of radiation from the metal enclosures. Servicemen have calibrated meters to check for radiation from the ovens.

Industrial use of radio frequency energy for heating is divided into two main categories. The first, used in heating metal objects, is called induction heating. Induction heaters employ a relatively high-power oscillator to generate radio frequency energy at low frequencies in the range of 10–400 kHz. These machines, like the medical diathermy machines, are now governed by design standards to ensure stable frequency and shielding to minimize interference with other services. The radio frequency energy is coupled to the workpiece by a coil and is capable of producing localized heat where desired. High-powered induction heaters can bring large slabs of metal to a red-hot heat. The process has been extremely useful in such applications as localized heat treatment of metal parts.

The other type of industrial radio frequency use is called dielectric heating. It finds wide application in the heating of materials of poor dielectric properties that can be quickly heated by the application of high-frequency energy. Dielectric heaters use fairly high frequencies or microwaves, as distinguished from the low-frequency induction heaters. Typical applications are in the manufacture of plastic garments where the seams can be welded by dielectric heating, and such products as plastic lamp shades.

Still another use of microwave energy is in burglar alarms and theft-protection systems. By flooding a given area with microwave energy any disturbance can be detected that will trigger an alarm. Theft-detection systems as used in retail stores and libraries operate on the principle of a small resonant inductor in the merchandise or book. On clothing a small device clips onto the garment and must be removed by the checkout clerk. If a person tries to take a garment out without paying, an alarm is sounded as the garment passes through the exit-detecting equipment. In libraries a small inductor is glued inside the book pocket that holds the due date card. When a book is properly checked out, the alarm will not sound. The checkout card is a laminated piece with a central layer of aluminum foil. This detunes the inductor and the alarm does not sound. Checking out without the proper card in the book pocket causes a disturbance in the microwave field and sounds the alarm. Book thieves have been known to tear out the pockets containing the inductor and thus disable the alarm.

One of the most innovative uses of radio waves is in astronomy. Very Long Baseline Array (VLBA) is a chain of radio telescopes linked together for coordinated observations. Due to the extreme length of the baseline, extremely high resolution can be obtained. The VLBA system was seven years in construction and cost $85 million. There are ten stations in the system and each one is identical, even to the floor plan of the buildings. Known technically as an interferometer, the system opened in May 1993 and has already achieved some spectacular results. Radio wavelengths used range from 7 mm to 90 cm, corresponding to frequencies from 43 GHz to 330 MHz. The following is a list of the VLBA observatory sites: Mauna Kea, Hawaii; Brewster, Washington; Owens Valley, California; Kitt Peak, Arizona;

Pie Town, New Mexico; Los Alamos, New Mexico; Fort Davis, Texas; North Liberty, Iowa; Hancock, New Hampshire; and St. Croix, U.S. Virgin Islands.

The VLBA was originally plagued with software problems in the computers that analyze the observed data. Despite these problems, Miller Goss, assistant director of the National Radio Astronomy Observatory, said in 1994, "The VLBA is now at the stage where we can get some real science out of it."

Another innovative use of radio frequency energy is "wired wireless," discovered in 1910 by George O. Squier (see biographies below). Squier held a doctorate in electrical engineering and later became chief signal officer of the army during World War I. Known more familiarly now as carrier current, this type of radio transmission involves coupling the transmitting and receiving apparatus to an existing wire circuit. Coupling capacitors are used to isolate the radio equipment from the wire. In this way radio communication can be carried on using a wire that may be carrying high-voltage electric power, or a working telegraph or telephone line. Relatively low power is needed for the radio equipment because the waves travel along the wire instead of being radiated through space.

Some of the early users of this equipment were the public utilities. When the nationwide electric power grid came into operation, a means of communication between the various electric stations was needed. Using carrier equipment connected to the high-voltage, cross-country transmission lines, this could be accomplished without the extra expense of dedicated telephone lines. These first power line carrier telephones employed AM-modulated equipment of rather conventional design operating on frequencies around 160 kHz or lower. The coupling circuits between the carrier set and the high-voltage line had to be carefully designed. The radio signal had to be coupled to the line, yet maintaining complete isolation from the high-voltage power. Also, the coupling network had to incorporate means of preventing the radio signal from being absorbed by the local power transformers. Power line carrier equipment eventually became very sophisticated in design and is used for remote metering and switching operations in addition to voice communication between stations.

Carrier was developed to a high degree by the telephone and telegraph companies for application to the open-wire, cross-country lines that were in widespread use prior to World War II. Carrier provided the means of adding many additional channels to a single pair of wires. In these applications the power and frequencies were usually lower than those normally employed in power line applications. The old open-wire telephone and telegraph lines were extremely efficient conductors of radio frequencies in the lower end of the spectrum. Supported on glass insulators with 8 or 12 inch spacing between wires, they had the ideal characteristics for radio frequency transmission.

When cables came into use, the problem of carrier current transmission was not so simple. Cables, made up of small conductors in close proximity, had much higher losses than open wire. The cables required closely spaced repeater stations to overcome the inherent losses. With improved filters it was possible to use lower carrier frequencies that could be transmitted with correspondingly lower losses.

In heavy industry, carrier-type equipment has been used for both voice communication and on-off signaling indications. In one instance such equipment was used on the charging cars used in the coke plant of a steel mill. The carrier equipment operated in the frequency range of 61–190 kHz. FM modulation was used for voice and frequency shift for the signaling applications. Power was derived from the 250 volt DC trolley rails. The same rails carried the radio carrier back to the control point.

Carrier principles have been employed in a wide variety of applications for home use. Sound distribution systems, remote telephone jacks, and intercom sets are among the devices used. They all work by coupling radio frequency energy into the electric power wiring of the home.

Long before television, when the Morse telegraph was state of the art for electrical communication, people were wondering if graphic images could be transmitted by wire. One of the first workers in this field was Alexander Bain. It was the same Bain who invented a chemical telegraph system that for a time was competing with Morse. Bain's telegraph operated by the action of electricity on chemically treated paper. When current flowed it made a mark on the paper. This enabled the transmission of dots and dashes by a code similar to Morse's. The Bain telegraph worked pretty well, but was subject to interference from other wires and finally lost out to the foolproof system of Morse.

Bain received a British patent in 1843 on his system of picture transmission. Another patent for facsimile transmission by wire was issued in 1905. However, not much was accomplished in the nature of practical application until the 1920s and 1930s when Bell system engineers started developing some practical apparatus. There was a great interest by newspapers and press associations in apparatus that would transmit by wire and radio not only facsimile images but also photographs that could be used for half-tone reproduction.

The machines involved scanning drums for both sending and receiving. At the sending end, the original picture to be transmitted was wrapped around the drum of the sender. At the receiver, sensitized paper was wrapped around the drum. Before starting to send, signals were transmitted that got both drums rotating in synchronism.

At the sender a light beam scanned each line of the picture and was translated into a signal that could be transmitted over wire or radio. At the receiver the paper was scanned by a light beam that varied according to the signals being received.

When the sensitized paper was developed it revealed a picture of the original. Once the technique had been perfected for transmission by wire, it remained only a matter of time until radio transmission had improved enough to make it possible to send pictures over the air. The first transatlantic radiophoto service opened on April 30, 1926. A photo was transmitted from London to the *New York Times* and published on May 1, 1926. The methods then used required 1 hour and 25 minutes to transmit the picture. RCA had a full page ad in the May 14, 1945, issue of *Time* to call attention to their radiophoto service. The ad pointed out the changes that had taken place since the 1926 photo transmission. By 1945 the time to transmit a picture from New York to London was down to around seven minutes.

The rotating drum method of scanning pictures was standard up to the time of World War II. As digital technology started developing after the war, the methods of transmitting pictures changed greatly. Probably the greatest step forward to improved methods came with the invention of the transistor in 1947. Now very complex circuits could be contained in compact equipment suitable for carrying anywhere in the world. Present-day photojournalists often travel with portable picture transmitters. They can develop their negatives and then place them in the transmitter. All that is needed is a good telephone line to the distant point to file the pictures. Physical telephone lines are now augmented by the so-called suitcase telephones that can access the worldwide telecommunications system from any location in the world. All that is necessary is to place the suitcase on a flat surface. The lid is opened and functions as an antenna that can be oriented to access the satellite signal.

Even cameras using regular photographic film developed chemically are on the way out. The new cameras scan the picture area and reduce the picture information to electronic bits that are recorded on a magnetic disk similar to those used with computers. Electronic cameras are available to amateurs now, but those who have tested them say the picture quality is somewhat below conventional cameras. The professional photographer, along with much more expensive camera models, presumably do a lot better and such equipment may soon become standard. No longer will the news photographer have to carry bulky rolls of film. All he will need is a supply of floppy disks to fit his camera. Besides speed, one advantage of the new methods is that they make it possible to enhance the original picture by electronic manipulation. The new methods are also much less vulnerable to interference or noisy transmission circuits. The old radiophoto circuits were especially vulnerable to interference on the particular channel used. Momentary interference could quickly make a picture unusable and then it was necessary to start all over again and hope that the interference didn't repeat while the picture was running.

Armstrong's invention of the superregenerative receiver in the 1920s was almost as sensational as his previous invention of the superheterodyne receiver during World War I. Much simpler in design than the superheterodyne, the superregenerative circuit was able to enhance the sensitivity of a single-tube receiver to a surprising degree. It was one of the first successful receivers of high-frequency signals and was the circuit used in many early police mobile receivers.

When Major Armstrong demonstrated the new radio before the Radio Club of America in 1922, he said, "What I have just shown you is a system that gives the same results with three tubes as you obtain with nine tubes in the superheterodyne principle. Now the superheterodyne is the Rolls Royce of radio, and while there are people who ride in Rolls Royces, there are quite a number who have to ride in Fords. Now I'm going to show you the Ford of Radio." In spite of the enthusiasm for the superregenerative receiver, it soon fell out of use due to some inherent defects. These defects were not so important in the early days of radio, yet they ruled out the use of the circuit under modern conditions. Among the limitations were radiation of a strong local signal from the receiver and the wide band characteristic of reception. The wide band characteristic was actually a benefit during the early years, but soon turned into a liability as frequency allocations became more precise.

•7•

On the Move

It was only logical that the first application of wireless, or radio, was to ships at sea. The ships were well adapted to the then primitive state of wireless. They had plenty of room to carry the bulky apparatus of the period, tall masts to string large antennas from, and were slow moving. At the turn of the century airplanes had yet to be invented and automobiles were still in an embryonic stage. As might be expected, the U.S. Navy was involved in the early development of radio. It was realized early that radio would be essential to all naval operations in the near future. The Navy Standard spark transmitter, and the SE-143 receiver were basic equipment on many ships in the early days. The primary emphasis was on telegraphic communication, but radiotelephony was not neglected. One of the first successful navy radio telephone sets was the CW-936 in 1918. This set had only 5 watts of power with a reliable range of 5 miles. Even with these limitations, the set proved quite useful for intercommunication between ships. The navy established some state-of-the-art shore stations to communicate with their ships. These navy stations also served the civilian maritime industry by transmitting weather reports, storm warnings, and time signals on a regular basis.

The navy operated the Naval Research Laboratory in the Washington, D.C., area. On the West coast research facilities were established at Point Loma, near San Diego, California. Point Loma had been the original location of one of the navy's long-wave stations using the call letters NPL. This station was established in 1906 and continued operation until June 1949 when it was decommissioned. The original transmitter at NPL was a 5 kw spark manufactured by the Massie Wireless Telegraph Company. The Point Loma laboratory was the first such installation on the West coast, established in June 1940 by Frank Knox, then the newly appointed secretary of the navy. The location atop Point Loma was considered optimal for experimental work in radio propagation and reception. Also, the nearness to the Pacific Fleet meant that the laboratory could readily support fleet needs.

Railroads, the main form of mechanical transportation, were highly developed but also steeped in tradition and not about to consider anything new, even if it was practical. Railroads cherished their Morse telegraph communications and block signal systems. There were some people however, who realized that as systems got more complex the old methods could not cope with the huge volume of traffic that was developing on major railroads.

On the Union Pacific railroad, Dr. Frederick Millener started experimenting with radio in 1906. By 1914 he announced that he had a commercially feasible device that would enable moving trains to communicate with stations 30 or 40 miles away. Tests of Millener's apparatus in 1916 were disappointing and a rather shortsighted committee report summed it up this way: "Even if the experiments had been a success, the expense would not warrant the Railroad Company in adopting the invention of Dr. Millener, due to the excessive cost and infrequent use." Prior to World War I, radio technology had not advanced to the point where communication with moving trains was practical. In this case the committee made the right decision. The Union Pacific had invested about $7,000 in radio experimentation, which was a large sum for that time. Union Pacific president W. M. Jeffers once declared bombastically that radio would never supplant telegraph dispatching on his railroad. However, before his death in 1953, Jeffers lived to see radio become an important part of railroad communications.

Even before the experiments with radio, the advantages of communication with moving trains had become apparent. As early as 1885 experiments had been made using the inductive system of telegraphing between trains and the trackside wires. This system had worked to some extent but was not suitable for large-scale application. It was not radio of course, being merely the inductive effect of a wire carrying current causing a reaction in an adjacent conductor. William Preece had used this method in England to communicate with offshore islands. The main disadvantage of the inductive system was that it was a one-channel system, so only one circuit could be operated in a given location without hopeless interference. A further disadvantage of the inductive system being applied to trains was the necessity to carry a Morse telegrapher on each train so equipped.

By 1927 radio was becoming more advanced and the General Electric Company was able to demonstrate voice communication between the engine and caboose of a train. This type of communication had some advantages but was not the total answer. What was needed was instant voice contact between the dispatcher and the train crew and between members of the train crew, even when some of them were working on the ground beside the tracks. Before radio, the sole communication between train crews was by hand signals in daylight and lanterns at night. Crews grew very adept at maneuvering trains around in response to hand signals but there were mistakes and accidents due to misunderstood signals. When the switchmen, brakemen, and conductors could give instructions to the engineer by means of handheld radios the whole operation became much more efficient.

Most of the early attempts at train radio involved amplitude-modulated sets operating in the frequency range just above the standard broadcast band. These frequencies were subject to atmospheric interference and were also subject to lack of efficiency due to the types of antennas that had to be used. After World War II, when frequency modulated equipment working around 160 MHz began to appear, the full potential of railroad radio started to emerge. Even though radios were becoming more practical, they had to combat problems that were not of a technical nature. Tradition-bound train crews, protected by union work rules, actually demanded extra pay for operating the radio. Eventually, of course, the train crews began to realize that the radio was the best tool they had and refused to operate without it. Design of equipment was constantly improving, both in reliability and compactness (photo 7.1). Some of the first radios intended for portable use by individual trainmen were rather bulky, shoulder-carried units. Now, compact handheld units answer most portable needs.

Railroads have developed their radio communication systems to a degree that surpasses anything that existed before World War II. Dispatchers now can converse at will with stations, trains, and individual crewmembers over a wide area. This is made possible by remote radio towers at intervals along the track so that even a handheld unit is within reliable communication range. Trackside detector units monitor passing trains and report by radio automatically. These trackside units monitor the number of axles on the passing train, the speed, and whether there is any loose, dragging equipment under the cars. With the traditional caboose now almost a thing of the past, most trains carry an end of train detector on the last car. This unit fits on the coupler of the last car and contains a radio transmitter that transmits the air pressure reading to the front of the train. Also, the unit emits a radio signal that alerts following trains that the track is occupied.

Radio technology started before the day of the automobile and the airplane, yet it lagged behind the progress made in those fields. We had practical airplanes and automobiles long before we had practical radio equipment to use in them. There were aircraft wireless sets in some World War I aircraft but they were elemental in nature and covered very short ranges. At that time, it was thought a great accomplishment if a military plane could communicate with ground units directly below. Some early specifications for aircraft radios called for a maximum range of 2,000 yards and if a range of 4 miles was achieved in tests it was thought exceptional. E. B. Craft of the

7.1. Trainman's shoulder pack radio made by Motorola (photo by Lewis Coe).

Western Electric Company once recalled some of the problems encountered in developing the first aircraft radio sets as follows:

> But working this apparatus under ordinary conditions on the ground, and in a swift moving and tremendously noisy airplane were two entirely different propositions. The noise of the engine and rushing air was such that it was impossible to hear one's own voice, to say nothing of the weak signals of the telephone receiver. One of the first problems was to design a head set which would exclude these noises, and at the same time permit the reception of the telephone talk. A form of aviator's helmet was devised with telephone receivers inserted to fit the ears of the pilot or observer. Cushions and pads were provided for adjusting the receivers to the ears, and the helmet fitted close to the face so as to prevent as far as possible, the sound being heard either through the ear passages, or through the bony structure of the head, which acts as a sort of sounding board. A helmet was finally developed and found to solve this portion of the problem.

Considerable work was also necessary to design a microphone for aircraft use. Planes of the early twentieth century were of the open cockpit variety and the same noise that plagued reception was picked up also by any ordinary microphone. It was necessary to devise a microphone that was insensitive to the noise frequencies yet that would respond to voice frequencies.

When Charles Lindbergh was flying the air mail from Chicago to St. Louis in the 1920s he had no radio at all. A compass, map, and a little luck were his only navigational tools. One youngster along the Chicago–St. Louis route took pity and mounted a powerful electric light on top of his parents' home. He wrote to Lindbergh that he would keep the light burning every night to mark the route. Lindbergh did not carry radio at all when he made his historic Atlantic flight in 1927 in his *Spirit of St. Louis*. Even the radio gear carried by the Lindberghs on some of their later survey flights was primitive compared to that carried by even a small private plane today. On the flight to the Orient in 1931 the plane was equipped with only a radio telegraph transmitter of 15 watts power. On this flight the Lindberghs arranged to leave the key down on the transmitter at all times when the plane was aloft. In this way observers could listen to the steady carrier and know that all was well with the flight. On the flight from Africa to South America in 1933 the equipment was scarcely better than the usual amateur radio station set. The receiver used plug-in coils for the various frequency bands and Ann Lindbergh was required to master Morse code to communicate with passing ships. In addition, Mrs. Lindbergh had to cope with the trailing wire antenna and remember to reel it in before landing. The trailing wire was the only way to mount an antenna on the relatively small aircraft that would give effective radiation on the frequencies employed. The Pan American radio equipment they carried would operate on the low frequencies of 333 and 500 kHz for communication with ships, and 3,130, 5,615, 8,450, and 13,240 kHz for contact with distant shore stations.

Other historic flights in the early days of aviation had no radio at all, or at best radio with limited capability. This was primarily because the radios of the day were bulky and heavy and tended to be unreliable in performance. Experienced pilots preferred to save the weight and complications of effective radio equipment. When a long flight was in progress the only reports came from visual sightings along the way. If the plane didn't arrive after it was known that its fuel supply was exhausted, the usual presumption was that it was lost with all on board.

When Commander Richard Byrd made his historic flight to the North Pole in 1926, his airplane, *Josephine Ford*, carried no radio. Waiting at Spitsbergen was the crew of the airship *Norge*. The first news of the successful completion of Byrd's flight came when one of the Italians burst into the mess hall and shouted, "She come — a motor!" The 1928 transarctic flight of Hubert Wilkins and Carl Eielson was undertaken to once and for all establish whether there were unknown land masses in the vast Arctic Ocean.

Their plane did carry a radio, but only a transmitter. A schoolteacher at Point Barrow had the mating receiver and he was to listen for reports from the plane. For a time the transmitter on the plane, operating on 33.1 meters, was heard at Point Barrow. Then the wind-driven generator that powered the transmitter on the plane failed and no further transmissions were possible.

Nothing more was heard from the flight until they finally arrived at Green Harbor near Spitsbergen after a series of misadventures. There was a wireless station at Green Harbor and they were able to report their safety. Since a prime objective of the flight was to report any land masses seen enroute, Wilkins had made up a code to report his findings to Dr. Isaiah Bowman of the American Geographical Society. The code involved various combinations of the word "foxes." After arriving at Green Harbor, Wilkins sent his historic message to Dr. Bowman, "no foxes seen." Thus the historic flight had established that there were no unknown land masses in the Arctic Ocean.

When Pangborn and Herndon made their 4,558 mile nonstop flight from Japan to the United States in 1931, they carried no radio at all. They had even arranged to drop the landing gear at sea after they were aloft in order to save weight. Their safe arrival on the West coast of the United States was confusing to watchers at the Wenatchee, Washington, airport because the plane came from the east instead of the west. This was because Pangborn had originally intended to make a landing at Spokane, only to find that airport fogbound. He needed clear weather to minimize the hazards of the belly landing.

The original radio navigation system for aircraft was the radio range starting in the 1930s. In this method highly directional antennas transmitted beams along the major routes. The nature of the beam was such that a pilot hearing a steady tone knew he was on course. If he strayed to one side of the course, he heard the letter "A" in Morse code and on the other side of the course he heard the letter "N." This system worked fairly well, given the low-altitude flight patterns of the time. Since it was done on low frequencies between 100 and 400 kHz, atmospheric noise was always a problem in summer. These same low frequencies are still in use today but for a different purpose. Now, a series of nondirectional beacons (NDBs) are spaced along the airways (see photo 7.2). The NDBs are designed to have no directional characteristics and serve merely as locators and can be used for obtaining bearings by radio direction finders if desired. Pilots today have a wealth of navigational information available compared to the old "A–N" beams, including radar, LORAN (Long-Range Navigation), and the global positioning receivers that are controlled by satellites.

Another system of radio navigation is called OMEGA. This system embodies a series of high-power transmitters operating in the range of 10 to 13 kHz. Unlike LORAN, there are no master or slave stations: each transmitter stands alone as a source of navigational information. The stations are located as follows: Norway; Liberia; Hawaii; North Dakota; La Réunion; Argentina; Australia; and Japan. Each station sends a series of 8 pulses in a 10 second interval. Overall accuracies of the order of one mile can be obtained even at extreme ranges of 5,000 miles. Transoceanic airlines have found OMEGA a good alternative for the more expensive inertial systems of navigation.

The VHF omnirange beacons (VORs) are spaced along the airways (see photo 7.3). These beacons emit a signal in the 108 MHz

7.2. Nondirectional beacon (NDB) at Wanatah, Indiana, transmits on 212 kHz with call sign "VP" in Morse code (photo by Lewis Coe).

range and transmit both voice and Morse code identifiers. Many VORs have voice transmission capability controlled by a flight service station. This enables direct voice contact between a flight service station and a pilot flying in the vicinity of a VOR.

An additional aid to navigation is provided by the Tactical Air Navigation (TACAN) equipment. Combinations of VORs and TACAN are called VORTAC. The TACAN equipment operates on a total of 126 channels in the UHF band. Transmissions from the VORTAC station are in the range of 962–1,024 or 1,151–213 MHz. The associated DME radio in the aircraft transmits in the range of 1,025–150 MHz. Most planes carry distance measuring equipment (DME), that can be tuned to a VORTAC along the route to give a readout of the distance and the estimated time of arrival. At high altitudes the VORTAC can give range information out to 195 nautical miles. Accuracy is typically plus or minus 720 feet at 10 nautical miles from the ground station.

Domestic flights carry voice frequency radios that operate in the 108 to 136 MHz aircraft band and use amplitude modulation (AM). Even though frequency modulation (FM) is used for most radio communication today, AM has remained in use for aircraft. The reason given is that AM has certain

7.3. VOR transmitter near Knox, Indiana, transmits Morse code identifier "OXI" on a frequency of 115.6 MHz (photo by Lewis Coe).

advantages when dealing with weak signals. Prior to World War II, the standard radio equipment on small aircraft was a small transmitter and receiver operating on 3,105 and 6,210 kHz. Commercial planes had higher-powered sets operating on proprietary channels also in the HF band of frequencies. War time developments in VHF and UHF equipment and the invention of the transistor made the present VHF sets on 108 to 136 MHz possible and greatly improved the quality of communication.

The invention of the transistor in 1947 brought about many changes in the design of equipment for aircraft. The equipment is much more compact and efficient. Even small private planes can carry duplicates of the radio sets to safeguard against failure of one unit. Cross-country flying is almost impossible today without functioning radios aboard. International flights today, in addition to the standard complement of radios carried by the domestic flights, depend on powerful single sideband sets when on transoceanic crossings. Single sideband is a form of AM in which the carrier and one sideband is removed, resulting in much higher efficiency for a given power. A normal amplitude-modulated signal consists of the carrier wave and upper and lower sidebands. All the speech information is in one sideband and thus the carrier can be tuned out at the transmitter and reinserted at the receiver. Most large commercial planes have a selective calling system on their radios. This means that the pilot is not distracted by continual chatter on the radio. The flight controllers can call up the desired plane by transmitting a coded audio signal. All aircraft are required to carry emergency locator transmitters (ELTs). These are low-powered, battery-operated units operating on the international emergency frequencies of 121.5 and 243.0 MHz. These transmitters are activated automatically if an airplane crashes and immediately start sending out a characteristic siren-like signal. By means of radio direction finders it is possible to locate downed planes in densely wooded or mountainous areas where visual sighting might be difficult. ELTs are sometimes activated accidentally by a rough landing or other causes and start sending out false signals. This inconvenience is considered to be minor when weighed against the value of the locating signal in a real emergency.

In addition to the normal voice communication, commercial airliners can be equipped with digital radio transmission systems. Called ACARS (Aircraft Communications Addressing and Reporting System), this equipment enables high-speed transmission of written data to and from planes. This reduces the volume of messages formerly sent over the voice system, and so is seen as quite an advantage in making that voice system more available for the needs of inflight navigation.

Broadcasting was well established and automobiles were in widespread use before radios in cars became very practical. At the present time it would be hard to sell a car that was not equipped with at least a radio. However, until the 1930s it was just not very practical to have a radio in a moving automobile. The technology of that time still required connection to a rather large antenna for satisfactory reception. The early vacuum tubes did not have much amplification, or gain, as compared to the later versions. This made it difficult to build a sensitive receiver in compact form. As vacuum tubes improved, automobile radios started to appear. The problem of power supply for the radio still posed some obstacles: the vehicle battery could supply the voltage for the tube filaments; and the "B" or plate supply had to be furnished by blocks of dry-cell batteries, just as was done with home receivers. Finally, the vibrator type of power supply solved the problem of the "B" voltage. Vibrators generated a pulsating voltage that could be stepped up by a transformer and rectified into direct current. The main problem with some of these early automobile radios was the high current drain. With typically 6 tubes and the vibrator power supply, a set drew 3 or 4 amperes from the car battery. Extended listening with the engine not running often resulted in a low battery.

The first sets with push-button selection of stations were hailed as a great improvement over the old tuning dials. The invention of the transistor in 1947 opened a whole new chapter in automobile radio. Compact sets no larger than a cigar box were sensitive enough to give satisfactory reception on a short whip antenna. Current drain of the new sets was only a fraction of that when vacuum tubes were used. There was no longer any need to shut off the radio when stopping the engine. Concurrent with the development of better car radios was the progress in eliminating ignition noise. One of the first problems that had surfaced in operating a car radio was the high noise level from the ignition. This noise was produced by the spark plugs that merrily generated Hertzian waves in the same manner as Marconi's first transmitter. Special design of spark plugs and the rest of the electrical system of the automobile was necessary to eliminate this annoyance.

· 8 ·

Military Radio

When the United States entered World War I, radio was almost in an embryonic stage compared with later developments. The army radio equipment of 1917 worked on the low-frequency bands where atmospherics were a problem. The vacuum tubes were the early types with limited gain and the equipment tended to be bulky and relatively inefficient. Aircraft radio was virtually nonexistent and could scarcely do more than communicate with ground stations directly below. Considered as state of the art was an aircraft radio tested in May 1917 that was credited with a 2,000 yard range.

Even before World War I, there were attempts to use radio for military communication, notably in the Second Boer War of 1899–1902. Radio at this time was still in a very primitive stage, but the requirements for communication in South Africa were urgent for both sides. The British, in particular, had several besieged garrisons with no means of communication with the outside world except heliograph signals by day and naval searchlights by night. Prior to the war, South Africa had a well-developed Morse telegraph system linking the various cities. However, much of it fell an early victim to wire cutting by the Boer commandos. Marconi sent out from England several sets of equipment for use by the British Army. The army had little success with the equipment and it was finally turned over to the navy. The navy had better luck and was able to communicate over distances up to 85 kilometers using ships in the Delagoa Bay Squadron.

The Boers had ordered six wireless telegraph sets from Siemens and Halske on August 24, 1899. Paying £110 sterling for the apparatus, they expected to use it for communication between the fortifications around Pretoria. Unfortunately for the Boers, the shipment was impounded by customs in Capetown and never reached the battlefield. Some of the original wireless equipment is preserved by Signal Formation Headquarters in Pretoria, South Africa.

After the First World War developments were rapid. The short-wave, high-frequency bands were emerging as the preferred medium for military communication, and the radios themselves were starting to be more compact and efficient. Even by the 1930s however, many shortcomings were becoming apparent in military radios. Continuing its love affair with the horse, the army still relied on equine transportation for field radios.

In the artillery, the traditional method of communicating with forward observers was to lay field-telephone wire to the location needed. This was slow and could not always keep pace with advancing troops. A retired officer recalls that in the early 1930s at Fort Sill, Oklahoma, the only radio available for communication with forward observers was the SCR-131. This was a heavy radio that required three men to carry it and several minutes to put in operation. Power was supplied by a hand-cranked generator. This radio originally operated on a frequency of 545–1,750 kHz, right in the broadcast band. Later versions operated on 4,000–4,360 kHz, a more practical frequency range for the military. In the later 1930s the artillery received some more portable radios for use by the forward observers.

Hand-cranked generators had their own story to tell. The military being what it is, the system ensured that the lowest rank in the unit was relegated to turning the generator. One private, who was quite a capable telegrapher himself, found that he was expected to crank the generator, while a second lieutenant, who barely knew the code, attempted to operate the radio. For all that, the hand-cranked generator was a good solution to the problem of operating a vacuum tube unit in the field. The necessary batteries would be heavy and have a limited life. But since there was always someone to turn the generator, radio operation could continue without limit. Then the coming of transistor radios largely eliminated the need for generators. Battery drain was minimal compared to the former tube-type sets. Relatively high power could be obtained from a set operating on a regular vehicular battery.

During World War I, there were some clever attempts to adapt existing technology to the requirements of field use (photo 8.1). The Germans had a portable arc transmitter powered by a 500 volt DC generator. The Americans even had a "horse-pack set" using a 0.25 kilowatt quenched gap spark transmitter, powered by a hand generator and using a crystal detector for receiving (photo 8.2). Some of these radios worked and at times performed useful service, but most of the time they had to yield to the more dependable wire lines using telephone and telegraph equipment. The period between World Wars was marked by steady improvements in radio equipment. Vacuum tubes were more sensitive, making it possible to design more compact and efficient equipment.

The decades between the wars were still linked to the vacuum tube. Even so, some remarkable progress was achieved in designing equipment with the components available. The BC-375 transmitter was a 100 watt unit that could be used for voice or telegraph operation on a wide range of

8.1. Operating a field radio station, Molliens-aux-Bois, France, June 1918 (photo courtesy National Archives, Still Pictures Branch).

frequencies. This set used bulky plug-in units for changing frequency ranges, yet it was a marvel of compact construction using standard components. This set was good enough that it served on many heavy bombers during World War II. Of course, it was pressed into service because there was nothing else available when the war started.

One GI, who served as a radio operator on a bomber, recalled his experiences with the BC-375 transmitter. It seems that the plug-in units for changing frequency were stowed in a rear location on the plane. To reach them it was necessary for the operator to traverse a narrow catwalk that was directly over the bomb bay of the plane. The operator recalled that it was a real adventure to change the coils, especially when the bomb bay doors happened to be open!

The so-called "command" series of transmitters and receivers was another example of late 1930 technology that was pressed into service because it was the only thing available. These command sets were a series of very compact transmitters and receivers built by the Western Electric Company. They employed conventional vacuum tube circuitry and were marvels of compact construction. Many were sold as surplus after the war and used to good advantage by amateur radio operators.

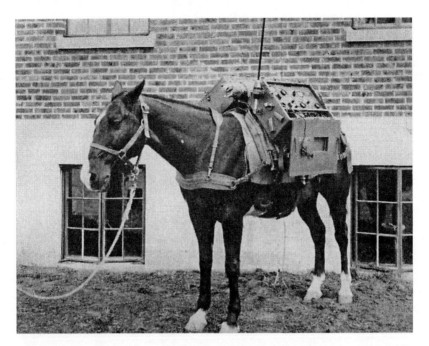

8.2. A horse pack radio set of the 1930s (photo courtesy National Archives, Still Pictures Branch).

The entire communication industry prior to World War II was geared to the vacuum tube technology. Some excellent tubes had been developed and there were even miniaturized versions that lent themselves to more compact construction. The invention of the transistor in 1947 was the high-water mark of military radio. Now lightweight, compact radios could be designed for every communication problem in the field or in the air. Military communication continues to progress with new developments that would have scarcely seemed credible to the soldiers of 1917.

The helmet radio used by the army during the Vietnam War is an example of how transistor technology made possible very lightweight and compact equipment (photo 8.4.). The receiver was a complete double conversion superheterodyne design, small and light enough to be worn clipped to the rim of the soldier's combat helmet. The receiver employed a small horn-type loudspeaker that directed the sound to the operator's ear without the necessity of wearing a headphone. In jungle fighting it was considered necessary that the operator's hearing not be impaired in any way by wearing an earphone. The companion transmitter was a compact unit that was handheld when in use and clipped to the belt when not in use (photo 8.5). These units were intended for short-range tactical use, generally within line of sight

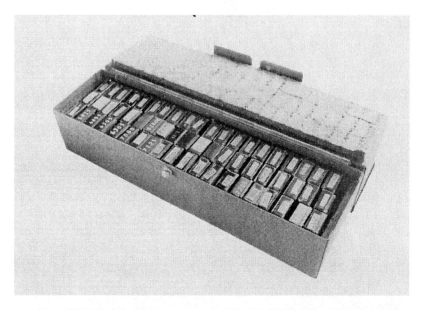

8.3. Crystal kit used for frequency control in World War II radio transmitter (photo by Lewis Coe).

range. They used FM transmission and reception in the 47–57 MHz range. The sets were operated by self-contained batteries and were crystal controlled on fixed frequencies. Reportedly not very well liked by the troops, the radios nevertheless represented a clever approach to a military communications problem.

At the farthest possible distance from the Morse telegraph networks of the Civil War is the army's new Mobile Subscriber Equipment (MSE). Military communication requirements have become increasingly complex. When a large army takes to the field they must take with them a communications system equal to that of a city of equivalent size. Military counterparts of civilian services must be provided and able to communicate with each other.

The MSE system is a high-speed digital network providing secure voice and data communications. It operates in somewhat the same manner as a cellular telephone system. When a call is initiated, it is automatically routed by the best available path to the destination. Problems were encountered in the first phases of MSE in that there was too high a rate of uncompleted calls. Improvements have raised the successful call completion rate to over 90 percent. The system can interface with wire lines and the various radio units found in a field organization. It is expected that five army corps will be equipped with MSE. The equipment of each corps will consist of 42 node

Top: 8.4. "Helmet radio" tiny receiver clipped to rim of combat helmet. Used in Vietnam War; *bottom:* 8.5. Helmet radio used in Vietnam War. Tiny receiver clipped to rim of combat helmet. Handheld transmitter carried on belt when not in use (both photos by Lewis Coe).

centers and 42 node center switches. All of the centers will be connected by radio links. The corps equipment will provide 92 radio access units and provide service to 8,200 wire line branches and 1,900 mobile radio units. The army feels that current plans for MSE will handle its communication problems until the year 2010.

Secure transmission has always been of the greatest concern to army voice frequency communication channels. Telegraph transmissions can be encoded but voice frequency communication has always posed a threat to security. A person making a voice transmission can inadvertently disclose some vital information. The problem of voice frequency security first became severe in World War I and continued into the Second World War. Among the efforts to make the voice channels secure was the use of American Indian code talkers to confuse the enemy.

The idea was originated during World War I by Captain E. W. Horner, who enlisted the services of eight Choctaws of Company D, 141st Infantry to transmit orders over the field telephone. The experiment was a success and the Germans were absolutely baffled by the American Indian tongue. The idea was revived during the Second World War. In this case, members of the Navajo tribe were chosen. The Navajos were chosen because there was a larger group of potential talkers to choose from. In addition, the Navajo language is considered the most difficult of the various Indian languages.

The idea of using the Navajos was conceived by Philip Johnston, son of a Protestant missionary. Johnston had grown up on a Navajo reservation and was fluent in the language. He took his idea to Major General Clayton Vogel, commanding general of the U.S. Marine Corps, Pacific Fleet, in 1942. Johnston brought four Navajos to Vogel's headquarters and had them stage a demonstration of translating English to Navajo and back again. Vogel obtained permission to recruit 30 men for a pilot project. A virtually unbreakable Navajo code was developed, taking advantage of the complexity of the Navajo language. Many arbitrary code words for military items were assigned. "Dive bomber" became *ginitsoh* (sparrow hawk). Grenades became *nimasii* (potatoes). Adolph Hitler was dubbed "Moustache Smeller," and Mussolini became "Big Gourd Chin."

The program was so successful that unlimited recruitment was authorized and the code talkers grew to a unit of 420 men. White recruits from the Navajo reservations could not be accepted because they spoke what was called "trading post language," which was not the same as the pure tribal Navajo tongue. One of the problems that developed was the fact that, due to the extreme secrecy of the mission, the Navajos were not allowed to communicate with their families. This precipitated many anxious inquiries from parents who could not understand why they had not heard from their son

8.6. SINCGARS field radio gives secure voice communication (photo courtesy ITT Aerospace/Communications Division).

in the Marines. The Navajo code was highly effective against the Japanese, most of whom had never even seen an American Indian, much less heard one speaking his native tongue. The Navajos have perpetuated their wartime heritage by forming the Navajo Code Talkers Association (103 West Highway 66, Gallup, NM 87301, telephone 1–505–722–2228).

Since field telephone conversations can sometimes be monitored by earth currents from closely spaced lines, it was always necessary to monitor our own communications almost as closely as that of the enemy. One method of foiling eavesdroppers that is being applied to field radios is the so-called "frequency hop" technique. In this method, the transmitter and its associated receiver are continually varied in frequency according to a predetermined plan. It is virtually impossible for an eavesdropper to monitor such channels unless he knows the key to the frequency hopping procedure. Known as SINCGARS (Single Channel Ground and Airborne Radio Subsystem), these radios are now in use by the U.S. Army and Marine Corps, and by other military organizations throughout the world (photo 8.6). They can also be adjusted to operate with conventional radios and to interface with the MSE network when required.

The basic radio can serve as a man-packed unit weighing about 16 pounds or be incorporated into a wide variety of ground vehicle or aircraft installations. Frequency range is from 30–88 MHz. These frequency hopping radios are extremely effective in countering enemy jamming. They were used in Desert Storm and have demonstrated as much as 7,000 hours of use before failure, an important military consideration.

Another version of the frequency hopping radio is called "Have Quick" and operates in the 225–400 MHz frequency band (photo 8.7). These radios

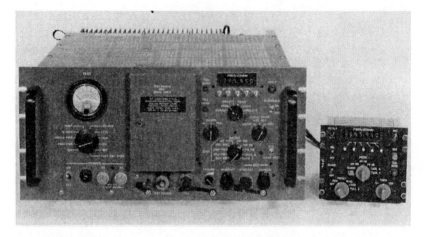

8.7. HAVE QUICK, a military radio designed for secure voice communication (photo courtesy of Rockwell/Collins Communications Division).

are considered virtually jam proof. A spokesman for Rockwell-Collins, one of the manufacturers of this equipment, explained it this way: "It makes it difficult to jam because the jammer doesn't know where you're going next. If he tries to jam the whole spectrum, he may jam you, but he's going to need a lot of power." Attempts to jam the whole spectrum makes the jammer vulnerable to retaliation because his position will be revealed.

As far back as 1914 the idea of frequency hopping had been advanced by the German Telefunken Company. With diplomats obviously concerned about the privacy of radio messages, the Germans said they could guarantee privacy with their system of simultaneous switching of frequency at transmitters and receivers. It has not been recorded that any such system ever was used. Now, with the great advances in technology, frequency hopping is entirely practical and widely used. At the time of World War I, radio technology had only been in existence for a scant 20 years. Yet the use of radio during the war was surprising, considering the equipment that we would now consider very primitive. Among the wartime developments was the superheterodyne receiver invented by Armstrong. The superheterodyne circuit is the basis of practically every radio receiver in use today. Although there were plenty of the old spark transmitters in use, vacuum tube sets were becoming available and they could be modulated for radio telephony as well as being far more efficient for telegraphy.

One type of equipment that had been made possible by improved receiving equipment was the radio direction finding set. Called goniometers, these sets took advantage of the directional characteristics of a loop antenna. Constructed of a number of turns of wire on a large wooden frame, the loops could be rotated to determine the direction a radio signal was coming from. Used primarily to determine the location of fixed stations, the direction finders yielded much valuable information about enemy activities. One gonio station at Menil la Tour set a record for operations during an attack on May 27, 1918. Three men operated the station and during a 24 hour period took bearings on 670 stations in one day.

The chief signal officer's report of 1919 tells of what was involved:

In order to take one bearing it is necessary to tune in the call-

8.8. Man pack version of SINCGARS radio. Provides secure voice communication (photo courtesy of ITT Aerospace/Communications Division).

ing station by manipulating the adjusting knobs with one hand while rotating a revolving frame with the other to find the two points of silence; in the meantime noting the call letters, time, points of silence, and figuring the mean of these, the wavelength and intensity of signals, and whether a message or call was sent, and in addition recording all this data. These men did this at an average rate of one every two minutes for eight hours each.

Goniometer stations were even able to pinpoint the location of radio signals emanating from aircraft. This capability was used to good advantage in locating enemy aircraft that were directing artillery fire. It was then possible to direct allied pursuit aircraft to the location of the hostile plane.

The underlying principle of all signal corps operations is that everything must be geared to the movement of troops. The radio tractors of World War I were one of the first attempts to give the army mobile communications centers that could keep up with the pace of combat. The radio tractors were originally equipped with 2 kw spark gap transmitters. Later, some

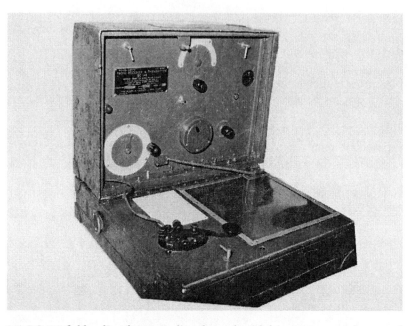

8.9. BC-148 field radio of 1936. Radio telegraph with loop antenna and powered by a hand cranked generator (photo by Lewis Coe).

of these units were rebuilt to include goniometer sets and continuous wave transmitters.

The basic idea of the radio tractors was continued in World War II. Heavy-duty vans carried a complete 500 watt radio station, capable of either voice or telegraph operation. The van towed a trailer containing a gasoline-driven generator to supply all the apparatus. Designated SCR-299, these vans were manufactured by the Hallicrafters Company of Chicago. Inside was an operating table with positions for two operators, duplicate receivers, and a BC-610 transmitter. The van was equipped with a vertical antenna that could be deployed to permit operations while in motion. The BC-610 transmitters used in these vans could be tuned to a wide range of frequencies by the use of quartz crystals and plug-in coil units (photo 8.3). These transmitters, sold as surplus after the war, became popular with amateur radio operators. Amateurs using the BC-610 transmitter were not too popular with television viewers. In the period after the war television reception was often marginal, and the BC-610 transmitter was not designed to minimize television interference.

A new technology that has been enthusiastically adopted by both the army and navy is the Global Positioning System (GPS). This enables any geographical location on the earth to be pinpointed with extreme accuracy.

Perhaps the first application was on ships and submarines where there was no problem in providing space and power for the apparatus. GPS depends on signals transmitted from a number of orbiting satellites and gives a direct readout in terms of latitude and longitude. Final developments have included handheld units not much larger than grandfather's old gold watch. Even these small units are surprisingly versatile. They have memory capability so that distant points can be entered in the memory and the device will plot the azimuth to the distant point. Survival

8.10. Soldier operating a mine detector of World War II vintage. Set operates on a radio frequency in the range of 280 to 330 MHz.

gear now carried by military pilots includes, among other things, a GPS receiver. Using this, a downed pilot can radio his exact position by means of the small battery-powered radio that is also included in the survival kit. The items of the survival gear are carried either in the pilot's vest or in the ejection seat that is activated in case an emergency exit is necessary.

Following a false armistice on November 5, 1918, the real one came on November 11, ending World War I. The U.S. Navy press sent the following dispatch detailing the terms of the armistice.

> Washington — November 11, 1918. Armistice signed by Germany effective six o'clock this morning Washington time and hostilities ceased. President Wilson at one o'clock read terms of armistice at joint session Senate and House. At same hour Premier Clemençeau read terms to French Chamber Deputies. Following proclamation given out by President this morning.
>
> "My fellow countrymen: the armistice was signed this morning. Everything for which America has fought has been accomplished. It

will now be our fortunate duty to assist by example, by sober friendly counsel and by material aid, in the establishment of just democracy throughout the world."

Terms of armistice include: immediate evacuation all occupied territory completed within fourteen days, including Alsace-Lorraine and Luxembourg. Evacuation left bank Rhine which Allies will occupy; will hold all principal crossings; surrender rolling stock in occupied territories. Bucharest and Brest treaties annulled; unconditional surrender all German forces East Africa; reparation for all damage done; withdrawal of all German troops from Russian, Turkish and Romanian territory.

Naval terms include immediate cessation of hostilities at sea and definite information given as to location and movements of all German ships. Notification to be given to all neutrals that freedom of navigation in all territorial waters is given to naval and merchant submarines of Allied and associated powers. Questions of neutrality being waived; all naval prisoners to be returned to Germany without reciprocity. Surrender of one hundred and sixty submarines in ports specified. All other submarines to be paid off and completely disarmed. Following surface ships to be disarmed and interned at neutral or Allied ports with only caretakers on board: six battle cruisers, ten battleships, eight light cruisers and fifty modern destroyers. All others to be concentrated at ports designated by Allies, paid off, completely disarmed, and placed under Allied supervision. Allies have right to sweep up all mine fields and obstructions laid by Germans outside German territorial waters, their positions to be indicated. Free access to the Baltic for Allied ships. To enforce this Allies to occupy all fortifications, all entrances from Cattegat to Baltic and to sweep all mines even in territorial waters. Existing Allied blockade to remain unchanged and German ships found at sea liable to capture.

All naval aircraft to be concentrated and immobilized at specified German bases. In evacuating Belgian ports and coasts Germany shall abandon all merchant ships, tugs, lighters, material for inland navigation, aircraft, arms and stores, etc. All Black Sea ports to be evacuated by Germans and Russian ships handed over to Allies to be returned without reciprocity. No destruction of ships or material to be permitted. German government to notify all neutrals restrictions placed on trading with Allies immediately cancelled. No transfer of German shipping to any neutral flag after signing armistice.

This lengthy message was transmitted by U.S. naval radio to all ships and shore stations. Thus concluded the war to end all wars.

•9•

Cellular and Satellite Telephones

The first mobile radio telephones offered by the Bell system operated around 150 MHz. They were bulky, trunk-mounted units in the automobile with a remote control mounted on the dash. The range was limited and there were few base stations outside of metropolitan areas. These first mobile telephones involved vacuum tube circuitry and dynamotor power supply for the transmitter. As such they imposed an extremely heavy drain on the vehicle battery, making it necessary to keep the engine running while the radio was turned on. Even with their limitations, the first mobile telephones were welcomed, especially by business and professional men who needed to keep in touch with their offices. Business men often advertised with pride that their cars were "radio equipped." The mobile phones grew in popularity to the point where the capacity of the existing service was taxed to the limit.

The Bell system of mobile phones was one of the first practical ones. However, there were attempts to provide two-way communication as soon as automobiles appeared on the road. One of the first, in March 1910, involved a transmitter using a ten-inch spark coil in the transmitter. Needless to say, this was purely a stunt, but it pointed the way to the future.

The so-called cellular system was developed to meet the expanding demand for mobile service. To provide more uniform coverage a much larger number of base stations or "cells" were constructed. The significant feature of the cellular system is the automatic transfer of the signal to the cell receiving the best signal as the mobile unit changes position. The other difference from the old system was the use of much higher radio frequencies: around 860 MHz. Besides improved transmission, it was thought that the higher frequency would provide more privacy than was the case with the 150 MHz frequencies that were covered by most home scanners. Newer scanners started covering the 800 MHz channels, and the telephone company was successful in getting a federal law passed that made monitoring radio telephone calls illegal. This didn't stop much of the monitoring, and the next step was to prohibit the manufacture or sale of scanners having the cellular frequencies on them. All of these measures were implemented in an attempt to convince users that their radio telephone calls were private. They aren't private, of course, in spite of all the laws and regulations.

As early as 1920 the telephone company was concerned about the problem of privacy using radio links to the public telephone system. The AT&T Annual Report in 1920 read as follows:

> The problem in attaining privacy in radio telephone transmission is peculiar and difficult. Nevertheless, in the solution of this problem we have also made important progress. Our engineers have carried on conversations by radio telephony according to a method which they devised whereby ordinary receiving stations can hear nothing but unintelligible sounds; yet at all stations equipped with the necessary special apparatus, and in possession of the requisite operating information, the spoken words can be heard and understood. Our development in this direction is being continued.

The system referred to above was the frequency inversion technique that was used on the first radio link to Catalina Island. Speech inversion of this type could be unscrambled by relatively simple home-built equipment. Later the telephone company used a so-called split band system to provide speech privacy. In this method the original speech frequencies were divided into five blocks of frequencies. These blocks were then juxtaposed in transmission so that only the special receiver could sort them back into the original order. Yet the telephone company likened all the privacy systems to the ordinary door lock: it keeps out the casual intruder but there is no way to keep the determined burglar out.

Since there is no actual privacy of communications using conventional FM radio equipment, the current trend among services requiring privacy is to use some form of digital modulation. This type of modulation, already in use by police departments and the military, is virtually free from unauthorized monitoring. It will probably be used eventually by all radio common carriers of speech communication.

There are thousands of the old scanners still out there and a clever technician can modify most of the new ones to receive cellular calls. There will always be people who find it an irresistible temptation to listen to other people's telephone conversations. Most of these listeners are motivated primarily by idle curiosity rather than any desire to derive any personal gain from the information they gain. The FCC is suffering from budget restraints

9.1. Satellite dish used for pickup of live television coverage from the cornfield scene of railroad wreck (photo by Lewis Coe).

and does not have the manpower to police unauthorized listening. If they did, it certainly would be possible to catch the illegal listeners. Scanners, like TV receivers and other radios, put out a tell-tale signal that can be heard at close range. TV rating services have used mobile receiving units that could cruise down a residential street and tell which TV channels were tuned in at various homes.

Purchasers of cellular phones must also sign up for the service before their phone is activated. Some services even give the telephone free to those who subscribe for a particular service. Cellular phones come in three basic types. Some are permanently installed in a vehicle; the so-called bag phones can be plugged into a vehicle cigarette lighter (bag phones are basically a vehicle phone installed in a portable case and have the advantage of more power than a handheld); and the handheld unit that has become the most popular type. With so many cellular phones circulating, they are now starting to appear in the used market. Persons who have discontinued the service are free to sell the instrument they used. A purchaser of one of these used phones must have it activated in his name if he wishes full service. Otherwise, a used phone will still give access to 911 service and can also be used to make credit card calls. The only thing it won't do is receive incoming calls. For persons who don't need full service a used phone can be a good buy just for the emergency calling feature. Needless to say, a used phone that is not in working order is not much of a bargain at any price. New phones sold without an activation agreement are usually prohibitive in price. This emphasizes the fact that what is being sold is service, not equipment. Buy a used phone as cheaply as possible, always anticipating that the batteries may need to be replaced before the phone will operate.

Cellular phones have assumed a new role in making people feel safer on the highways. The lone woman in a car knows that help is within easy reach if an emergency arises. Industry sources estimate that there are about 16 million of the cell phones in use, and of these some 70 percent of the users have them for safety reasons. Police in general are enthusiastic about the new uses of cellular phones in spotting dangerous drivers, the prompt reporting of accidents, and other aspects of public safety that have been enhanced by the proliferation of telephone-equipped cars on the road. It is estimated that presently people with car phones make as many as 600,000 calls per month to emergency numbers. The only down side to the wide use of the car phones is that certain individuals like to play cop and can get themselves involved in dangerous situations, and the 911 lines are being overused at times.

All of the telephone operating companies that offer cellular service find it one of their most profitable operations. This is because it doesn't cost much to add a new subscriber. Just a few key strokes on a computer does it: no stringing wires and making connections on distributing frames. Also cellular service is attractive to the operating companies because most cellular phone subscribers make a lot of calls. They are the kind of people who habitually have big phone bills. Cellular phone users who operate in their primary service area avoid many of the local toll calls that fixed subscribers must pay. When a cell phone goes outside of its district it becomes a roamer. Roamers pay extra charges depending on the rate schedules in effect for that area. If a fixed phone calls a roamer then the caller is billed for the toll charges that apply.

For some time cellular telephones have been offered as an option on automobiles. Taking this idea one step further, Ford is now offering an option on their 1996 Lincoln Continental models that combines cellular telephone capability with the Global Positioning System (GPS). If the driver of the car calls a 911 number in an emergency, the GPS equipment pinpoints the exact location of the vehicle and routes the call to the proper agency in the geographic area where the car is located. The GPS antenna is mounted on the trunk lid of the car. The driver of the auto can select one of two buttons to push in an emergency, one to summon a medical team and one to summon a tow truck for mechanical assistance (photo 9.2).

Among the newest communication miracles are the satellite telephones. These take advantage of the worldwide coverage of the INMARSAT communications satellites. These satellites are in geostationary orbit above the equator, positioned so that any spot on the globe can access them. Typical subscriber units are mounted in suitcase-sized containers weighing about 28 pounds (photo 9.3). Running on internal batteries, they can provide a telephone circuit from literally any place on earth. The antenna is built into the lid of the carrying case. It is only necessary to place the case on a flat surface and raise the lid. Built-in indicators allow rotation to get the best signal strength from the satellite. These units are probably too expensive for the casual user, but offer many advantages to the professional user where communication is essential regardless of the cost. These units operate on microwave frequencies 1,626.5

9.2. Typical cellular telephone base antenna (photo by Lewis Coe).

to 1,660.5 MHz to transmit, and 1,525.0 to 1,559.0 MHz to receive. The service offers full duplex, digitalized voice transmission as well as data transmission at 2,400 bps.

The suitcase-sized telephones of INMARSAT may eventually be upstaged by a new phone system. A satellite called MSAT, built by Hughes was launched in April 1995 and is positioned to provide North American coverage. Other satellites are planned to increase the coverage to worldwide. The equipment to access the new satellite is being built by Mitsubishi and Westinghouse and only weighs 10 pounds, considerably smaller and lighter than the suitcase-sized equipment. No antenna aiming will be necessary; only a clear view of the sky is required. These new phones are designed to use the existing terrestrial cellular network when within range and then switch to satellite when out of range of the cellular network. Cost is said to be as low as 75 cents per minute. MSAT users will have a single phone number with a special area code.

9.3. Suitcase satellite telephone provides a telephone circuit from anywhere in the world (photo courtesy Magnavox Electronics Systems Co.).

When it comes to radio, some of the pioneer scientists had uncanny vision concerning what the future might hold. Lecturing in 1897 before the Imperial Institute in England, Professor W. E. Ayrton spoke as follows:

> Some time the day will come, when we are all gone, when copper wire and gutta-percha cables will be seen only in museums; then a man who wants to talk to his friend and does not know where he is, will call him with an electrical voice. He will call "Where are you?" And only a man possessing a similarly tuned ear will be able to receive the call. The friend will answer "I am at the bottom of a coal mine near Newcastle," or "I am flying across the Andes," or "I am sailing across the Pacific." Perhaps no voice will reply. Then it is sure that the friend is dead.

Although Ayrton's prediction of 1897 is not quite a reality today modern technology is getting close to it. Several telecommunication companies are talking of a personal wireless telephone service that will work through satellites and allow the individual user access to the phone system wherever he may be. At present the problems are not so much technical as they are involved with corporate haggling over who is going to implement the new service.

When radio was the province of the Department of Commerce under Herbert Hoover, the underlying principle governing the allocation of licenses was "the public interest, convenience and necessity." Now the issuance of licenses seems to be governed by who has the most money. The FCC holds auctions in which valuable spectrum space is knocked down to the highest bidder. Once part of the unknown emptiness of the vast continent, the hot frequencies now are the ones used to access satellites and the microwave frequencies used for cross country communication routes. An article appearing in the *New York Times* on February 1, 1995, announced the FCC decision to award licenses to 3 companies to launch spacecraft and initiate a new era of radio telephone communication that would seriously rival the current cellular system. The companies involved are Iridium, associated with Motorola; Globalstar, a partnership between Loral and Qualcomm; and TRW. None of the new services is expected to be available before 1998.

The term wireless that was supposedly put to bed over 90 years ago is being revived in a big way. All of the new satellite telephone services are being advertised as wireless. Even the FCC has recently renamed its Private Radio Division. It is now called the Private Wireless Division. Apparently, the reason for the revival of the word wireless is that the public has grown used to the word radio. Using the word wireless may be the only way that attention can be directed to a service that is totally unlike any previously offered.

Satellite communication has become something that we almost take for granted and it has made possible services that were not even dreamed of 50 years ago. Yet these miraculous satellites are not exactly an unmixed blessing. Like any manmade device, they are subject to failure and it is not easy to send a repairman out to fix them when they go wrong. Ground-control stations can make adjustments and corrections but they cannot repair something that really breaks down. People who depend solely on satellites to conduct their business are always in danger of losing vital services. A case in point occurred in 1994 when Canadian news organizations lost one of two satellites used to service several Canadian papers, including the *Toronto Globe and Mail*. Fortunately, backup facilities had been provided. Some of the services had to be transferred to an alternate satellite and this required re-aiming of receiving dishes at several sites — not an easy thing to do on an emergency basis. The Canadian satellite failure was explained in this way by a Telesat spokesman: "Effects from the solar particle stream are the most plausible explanation we have." Such an explanation couldn't have been too reassuring to the users of the service. In all justice, it should be reported that these satellites had functioned with 100 percent reliability for 13 years before they gave any trouble (photo 9.1).

Another concern is the vulnerability of satellites to enemy action in case of war. We are literally depending on satellites for communications, navigation, and other services. Most of the old facilities using conventional radio transmission have been deactivated. Minimum domestic communication requirements could probably be met by existing cable and microwave networks. Cables are available for international communication as well, but their integrity could not be assumed in time of war. Loss of satellite links would severely cripple international services. Ironically, most overseas cables depend on satellites as backup in case of cable failure, which does occur periodically. Cable failures are a little easier to fix with modern cable ships, but they do require some time and are subject to weather conditions.

At the World Administrative Radio Conference (WARC) held near Malaga, Spain, in 1992 one of the hottest items on the agenda was the allocation of frequencies in the band from 1.5 to 2.5 GHz. These are the frequencies that will be used by many of the proposed wireless services. Some of these are now operational, others are still on the drawing board or mired down in corporate haggling. Wireless facilities are being proposed for many local networks that now operate by conventional wire links. With advancing technology making it possible to utilize ever higher frequencies, there seems to be no upper limit and frequencies as high as 60 GHz are currently being discussed. One of the intriguing possibilities being mentioned is the incorporation of wireless capabilities in the ordinary home computer, requiring a suitable antenna connection to the computer. This would mean that computers could actually go online with distant equipment without making any use of the public telephone system. Many computer users live in areas where there is no local telephone number for the various online services. This means that prohibitive toll charges will accumulate for any extended online activity. Contrary to popular opinion, a computer cannot communicate with anything unless it is connected to a telephone line linking it to the distant point. There will no doubt be some extra cost involved in using one of the projected wireless links, but it should be comparatively reasonable compared to public telephone interconnection.

AT&T has estimated that, by the year 2000, one billion users could be using wireless modems to participate in all sorts of computer activities. E-mail is skyrocketing in popularity and the wireless modems will make it available to more and more users.

·10·

Wireless Transmission of Power

Ever since the first disclosures of James Maxwell, wireless transmission of power has been the great dream. Yet it still remains an impossible dream, often hinted at, but remaining far beyond any technique now known. The basic principles so far have eluded the most advanced thinking. It will be left to a future Maxwell to scratch at the very edge of the unknown and point the way to what may someday become as commonplace as radio. The late Ernst Alexanderson, one of the most capable electrical engineers ever to practice in the United States, speaking in 1944 characterized radio as "the new fire which the gods have given to man." He mentioned that ultimate developments with the new fire might open the way to wireless transmission of power. Alexanderson did not elaborate on his remarks because he feared they would be misinterpreted. Nothing has ever happened along this line and wireless transmission of power remains the impossible dream. At the Century of Progress in Chicago in 1933 there was an exhibit purporting to show radio transmission of power. A small electric motor was displayed on a pedestal. The motor was running, and it could be lifted up from the table to prove that there were no wires connected to it. This was surely wireless transmission of power. Yet most viewers were unaware that a nearby curtain concealed a powerful generator of radio frequency energy. It was a stunt, pure and simple. It did illustrate, however, the utter impracticality of transmitting power using conventional generators of radio frequency energy.

Certainly the leading exponent of wireless power transmission was Nikola Tesla (1856–1943). Speaking before the American Institute of Electrical Engineers in 1891, Tesla prophesied as follows:

> Ere many generations pass, our machinery will be driven by a power obtainable at any point in the universe. This idea is not novel.... We

find it in the delightful myth of Antheus, who derives power from the earth; we find it among the subtle speculations of one of your splendid mathematicians.... . Throughout space there is energy. Is this energy static or kinetic? If static our hopes are in vain; if kinetic — and this we know it is, for certain — then it is a mere question of time when men will succeed in attaching their machinery to the very wheelwork of nature.

Tesla theorized that with his system of power transmission a very simple installation would be required to extract electrical power in useful amounts anywhere on earth. All that would be required was a radio frequency tuning unit, a ground rod, and an antenna pole to collect the energy that was passing through the air. Of course, Tesla was never able prove this theory or demonstrate it and neither has anyone else. The reason that it won't work is because it is based on the original theory of radio transmission for communication purposes. Here, only a minute voltage is sufficient to convey information to the receiver. The most powerful radio transmitters ever built could generate intense fields in the proximity of the station. Yet within a few miles they were merely radio signals, albeit stronger than some. It is all governed by the immutable laws of electromagnetic radiation. This law says that the strength of the field is inversely proportional to the square of the distance.

During 1899–1900 Tesla had established an experimental laboratory at Colorado Springs, Colorado. Here he conducted many experiments in high-voltage phenomena. He claimed to have generated voltages of 20 million volts with his apparatus, resulting in lightning flashes 135 feet long. His Colorado experiments had led some writers to claim that he had actually transmitted power sufficient to light a bank of 250 watts incandescent lamps at a distance of 26 miles. This was never claimed by Tesla himself and was pure fiction. He did say, however, "While I have not as yet actually effected a transmission of a considerable amount of energy, such as would be of industrial importance, to a great distance by this new method, I have operated several model plants which have thoroughly demonstrated the practicality of the system."

With Tesla's work occurring in about the same time frame as Marconi's, some authorities claimed that Tesla was the real inventor of radio. There is no doubt that Tesla's powerful spark discharges were creating Hertzian waves, but there seems to be no record that he actually used them in any sort of practical communications system as Marconi did. However, there was plenty of evidence that Tesla had conceived the basic idea of radio communication.

As early as 1893 he had given lectures outlining essentially the same ideas that Marconi patented four years later. Today the Tesla-Marconi controversy is almost forgotten and seldom mentioned in reference books. Tragically, Tesla died in January 1943, a scant six months before the U.S. Supreme Court affirmed his claim to be the true inventor of radio. The decision was handed down on June 21, 1943, in connection with a suit between the Marconi Wireless Telegraph Company of America and the United States (*United States Reports*, 320:1–80).

The suit arose out of the Marconi company's contention that the United States had allowed the production of equipment that infringed on the original Marconi patents. Those who wade through the 80-page document reporting the trial may be left wondering what it was all about. Boiled down to the essentials, it did affirm that Tesla had set forth the basic principles of radio communication before Marconi and others. Of course, Tesla died before this decision was handed down, but in his own mind he probably always thought as much anyway.

The late Haraden Pratt, fellow and past president of the Institute of Radio Engineers, was of the opinion that Tesla's ideas and theories were to some extent picked up and reduced to practical form by others. For this reason Pratt noted: "Tesla's influence on the development of radio was known to but a limited number of people. A few eminent persons who attended or read his lectures during the 1890 decade were inspired by his revelations and some others, who later delved into the background of the art, became aware of the pioneering import of his contributions." In a paper published by the IRE *Proceedings* in 1956, Pratt wrote as follows:

> Far ahead of his time, mistaken as a dreamer by his contemporaries, Tesla stands out as not only a great inventor but, particularly in the field of radio, as the great teacher. His early uncanny insight into alternating current phenomena enabled him, perhaps more than any other, to create by his widespread lectures and demonstrations an intelligent understanding of them, and inspired others not yet acquainted with this almost unknown field of learning, exciting their interest in making improvements and practical applications.

Writing in *Electrical World and Engineer* in March 1904, Tesla detailed the principles of radio communication in a way that was considered the best exposition of the subject at that time.

> World Telegraphy constitutes, I believe, in its principle of operation, means employed and capacities of application, a radical and fruitful departure from what has been done heretofore. I have no doubt that it will prove very efficient in enlightening the masses, particularly in still uncivilized countries and less accessible regions, and that it will

add materially to general safety, comfort, and convenience, and maintenance of peaceful relations. It involves the employment of a number of plants, all of which are capable of transmitting individualized signals to the uttermost confines of the earth. Each of them will be preferably located near some important center of civilization, and the news it receives through any channel will be flashed to all points of the globe. A cheap and simple device, which might be carried in one's pocket may then be set up anywhere on sea or land, and it will record the world's news or such special messages as may be intended for it. Thus the entire earth will be converted into a huge brain, capable of response in every one of its parts. Such a single plant of but one hundred horse-power can operate hundreds of millions of instruments. The system will have a virtually infinite working capacity, and it must needs immensely facilitate and cheapen the transmission of intelligence.

Tesla's great contribution to electrical science was his development of the polyphase alternating current motor. His association with George Westinghouse was the basis for the development of the alternating current power distribution system that has been the standard for many years. One of Tesla's first jobs in the United States was with Thomas Edison. The two had a misunderstanding that resulted in Tesla leaving in a huff. Later Tesla and Edison were in a head-to-head confrontation over the merits of Edison's direct current power system and the alternating current system of Tesla and Westinghouse. Edison stubbornly held to the merits of his DC system. The Edison group even held public demonstrations in which small animals were electrocuted with alternating current. They used the term "westinghoused" to describe the electrocutions. All of this was intended to scare the public into avoiding the use of alternating current electricity. Even though Edison was finally forced to concede the superiority of the AC system, his DC system held on for a long time. As late as the mid–1950s there were Edison DC plants still operating in certain districts of Chicago, New York, and other large cities. The disadvantage of the DC system was that it was not adapted to nationwide power distribution as we have today with the AC system. Tesla's alternating current system was used at the Niagara Falls power plant that opened in 1895. He predicted as early as 1890 the future use of electrical energy for induction and dielectric heating and the use of medical diathermy.

Tesla's Colorado Springs experiments were spectacular, but did little to enhance his dream of wireless transmission of power. His final effort in this direction was the tower he erected on Long Island, New York, at a place called Wardenclyffe. The 200 acre site was located near the town of Shoreham on the northern shore of Long Island in Suffolk country. Ironically, it was not far from the later location of RCA's Rocky Point transmitting station that was truly a "radio central."

Standing 200 feet high with a 70 feet metal dome on top, the Wardenclyffe tower was intended to be a world communication center. Whether Tesla had any clear idea how he would accomplish this is not known. Tesla ran into financial difficulties long before the tower was completed and he was unable to obtain further financing from his backer, J. P. Morgan. Morgan had advanced $150,000 and stated in the beginning that this amount was as far as he would go. The whole project finally came to a grinding halt. The tower was torn down and the materials sold for scrap to raise money for creditors' claims. If all of this sounds fantastic today, remember it was 1900. Radio was a mysterious subject to most people. Marconi himself was still struggling to achieve reliable communication over modest distances. The famous letter "S" transmission across the Atlantic was a very marginal achievement and only gave a promise of what might lie ahead.

In his later years Tesla became increasingly controversial. He issued all sorts of extravagant claims, none of which he could back up with any proof. His turbine, for which he vainly sought development capital from J. P. Morgan, was never successfully manufactured in the inventor's lifetime, mainly because there was no known metal that would stand the stresses imposed by the high rotational speed. Living out the final years of his life in a luxury suite at the Waldorf-Astoria hotel in New York, he was in continual financial difficulties. The once substantial income that he enjoyed had been dissipated over the years and there was no new money coming in. His main occupation in the final years was feeding and caring for the pigeons that flourished in New York. Even so, he continued to issue startling pronouncements of scientific achievements that never materialized. Most of Tesla's notes and records were sent back to his native Yugoslavia. Other records are supposedly in highly classified government files in the United States. For these reasons it may be a long time before the full scope of Tesla's work is known and appreciated by the public.

Even though Tesla's dream of wireless power transmission seems to be farther away than ever, it continues to inspire scientists who search for a practical way of accomplishing it. Richard Dickinson, head of the Microwave Power Transmission project for Cal Tech's Jet Propulsion Laboratory, says he has been inspired by the early work of Tesla. He described one experiment of the mid–1970s thus: "We beamed power from our transmitter at Goldstone a distance of one mile. All of the microwave energy that fell within our target, we converted 82.5 percent to useful direct current. Thirty-four thousand watts of direct current output carried a distance of one mile. We are well pleased."

This and other experiments suggest that, while power transmission by radio may be possible, it is a long way from being practical. A more practical derivative from Tesla's early work is seen in the navy's ELF communication project. By using extremely low frequencies around 80 Hz and extremely long antennas it has been possible to send one-way messages to submarines submerged in deep water. This system is considered to be worth the cost because it is possible to signal nuclear submarines to rise to the surface and establish two-way communication by satellite radio.

If talk of wireless power transmission seems unrealistic today, it should not be discounted for the future. One only needs to realize what skepticism would have greeted those who prophesied in 1900 the present developments in radio, television, aircraft, automobiles, and moon landings. Who can say that the great dream of wireless power might not be realized in another 50–100 years?

However, it is certain that whoever makes the breakthrough will go down as one of the great figures in scientific history. Imagine a countryside uncluttered with poles and wires. Not only are utility lines a cosmetic nightmare, they are expensive to build and maintain. Subject to weather, wild-driving motorists, and other hazards, the pole lines are one of the weak links in the power chain that we all depend on. It only takes a power failure on a cold winter day to make us wish that there was something better. Samuel Morse had a great idea when he proposed to bury the first Washington–Baltimore telegraph line underground. Morse's only problem was that no one knew how to make a good underground cable. Forced to string his telegraph line on poles, Morse unwittingly set the pattern for electric power distribution.

The only exception came in large cities where sheer congestion in the air space over the streets forced electric companies to run their wires in underground conduits. Next to rebel against the proliferation of overhead wires and poles were the residential subdivisions. Better cables were being manufactured and innovative new techniques developed for underground distribution of electrical service. Today it is rare to find a new residential area that does not have a complete underground system. Cross-country lines in rural areas are another story. There are few areas of the country that are not disfigured by a growing complex of wires, poles, and steel towers. The utility companies have been able to do this because the public demands more and more electrical power. Even though the technology now largely exists to place all lines underground, the utility companies argue that such a move would be prohibitively expensive. They say that electric rates would rise sharply and most consumers are dedicated to opposing rate increases, regardless of the reason.

One only needs to look at the telephone industry to see the benefits of underground construction. Of course, the telephone company had a somewhat simpler problem due to the nature of their lines. Telephone lines work at much lower voltage and the problems of designing suitable underground cables are a lot simpler than when dealing with extremely high voltages. Nevertheless, it was only a few years ago that most roads were cluttered with telephone lines and poles in great number. First, the telephone companies substituted aerial cable for the open wire lines. Then they buried the cables so the poles are rarely seen anymore. The change came so gradually that most people didn't even notice anything. They would certainly notice if those poles and wires all came back! Aside from the cosmetic improvement, the telephone system is now largely independent of weather conditions and lightning strikes. The increased cost of the underground lines has probably largely been offset by the decreased maintenance costs as compared with the old system. In the above-ground days it was necessary to station regular patrolmen along important stretches of lines at about 50 mile intervals. Only in this way could the lines be protected against the day-to-day minor problems that always developed. Needless to say, this was expensive.

The only alternative to the present power distribution system is the idea of transmitting power by direct current. This idea, which was first considered at least 60 years ago, involves converting high-voltage alternating current to direct current for transmission. At the destination the direct current is converted back to alternating current for local distribution. Over the years several experimental lines have been put in operation using this system. However, the disadvantages seem to outweigh the obvious advantages, and the present power distribution grid is an alternating current system as originally designed by Tesla.

In 1935 a team from the General Electric Company engaged in intensive research on direct current power transmission. The team included Alexanderson, of alternator fame, whose name crops up in many discussions of electrical matters. The GE team reported their work at the Winter Convention of the AIEE in 1935. Further information was published in the *General Electric Review* of May 1936. The whole subject of direct current power transmission as it then existed was summarized as follows:

1. It is a constant-current direct current system.

2. It is a system where the power flow is in one direction only at the will of the operator; but the power can be transmitted in either direction if desired.

3. The amount of power flow is under the control of the operator at all times.

4. No wattless power is transmitted.

5. A short circuit on any circuit of this type results in a reduction of power flow on the circuit involved.

6. Power can be transmitted by either overhead or underground lines any distance desired.

7. A circuit of this type can be tapped at any point to furnish power or to take power.

8. The nature of the circuit is such that systems of like or unlike frequencies can be operated together to feed any other system of like or unlike frequencies.

9. Overhead systems of this type should be more reliable, and less disturbance will be caused by lightning.

10. The system cannot become out of phase or out of synchronism with the system feeding it or with the system receiving power.

Even with the obvious advantages of direct current transmission, it has seen little practical use beyond the experimental lines. Aside from problems of insulator flashover, direct current power transmission has never been widely used due to the probable increased costs, and the normal tendency to remain with what is working and well understood.

·11·

Television

After the miracle of wireless transmission of Morse code messages through space, the next step was transmission of the human voice. Progression in radio was much the same as it had been in the telegraph and telephone art that came before. First came the transmission of Morse code and then finally the great achievement of the telephone. As soon as transmission of voice and music had been accomplished over radio waves a few visionaries started thinking that maybe in some way the new medium could transmit visual images. The public, of course, was absorbed in the new and rapidly escalating broadcast boom and that was enough to hold the popular fancy for several years. Nevertheless, a few dedicated workers were pushing toward the transmission of visual images. Accounts of their work appeared in *Radio News* and other publications during the 1920s. These early accounts of television experiments were for the most part skipped over by readers eager for the latest details on broadcast receivers that they could build or buy.

Early efforts at television transmission centered on mechanical scanning disks. Large, circular disks were drilled with a series of holes in a spiral pattern. As the disks turned, light shining through the holes scanned the picture. Essentially, the same thing is now done electronically. There were many shortcomings to the mechanical scanning system. The received image was very small and even when viewed through a magnifying lens was still relatively small and indistinct. Today even a portable five-inch TV receiver is far superior. Those early receivers only gave a vision of what might be coming in the future. The dedicated workers in the field realized that something better had to be devised if television was ever to exceed radio in popularity.

Developments in cathode ray tubes, in which an electron beam could be focused on a phosphorescent screen in a predetermined pattern, paved the way for the invention of fully electronic television. One of the most gifted inventors to work on television in the early days was Philo Farnsworth

(1906–71; see Appendix I). As a boy, growing up on a remote farm in Utah, he had demonstrated an unusual talent for science. Aided and encouraged by parents who understood his ambitions, young Farnsworth at age 16 had outlined to his high school instructor the basic design of a television system. Becoming one of the most important and respected researchers in the field, he secured two patents in 1930 that covered the essential features of modern electronic television.

Patent interferences between Farnsworth and the RCA inventor, Dr. Vladimir Zworykin, resulted in a lengthy court battle that was eventually won by Farnsworth. Before they became court room adversaries, Zworykin had been invited to witness a demonstration of the Farnsworth system. The three-day demonstration occurred April 10–13, 1930. After it was over, Zworykin said, "This is a beautiful instrument. I wish that I might have invented it." RCA was then forced to pay Farnsworth $1 million for the rights to use his invention, which was essential to the development of television as we know it today. Sadly, many historical accounts tend to ascribe the invention of TV solely to RCA's Zworykin, completely ignoring the great contributions of Farnsworth. In 1983 Farnsworth was honored by having his likeness placed on the 20 cent U.S. postage stamp in the American Inventor series.

After the basic method of electronic television had been worked out, there still remained the problem of how best to deliver the picture to the home viewer. It had been early recognized that the transmission of video and the accompanying audio signal would require more frequency space than could be accommodated in the radio channels then in use. The radio frequency spectrum, once thought to be inexhaustible, was already crowded with broadcasting, marine radio, and a host of other services. Development of radar during World War II had brought about intensive research in the utilization of the very high (VHF) and ultra high (UHF) frequencies above 30 MHz and it was in this part of the radio spectrum that postwar TV channels were assigned.

VHF and UHF transmissions are normally limited to line-of-sight ranges, and in the beginning many parts of the United States could not receive TV transmissions. Eventually, as more local stations came on the air and cable distribution systems were installed, the coverage was almost complete. Today, with the use of satellite equipment, there is virtually no part of the earth that cannot be reached by television. Initially, it was thought that by staggering channel assignments between regional stations that the channels could be repeated across the country. Occasionally, changing propagation conditions — particularly on the VHF channels — have resulted in serious interference problems.

One of the problems inherent in placing the TV channels in the

VHF-UHF portion of the spectrum was the designing of tuners to cover this frequency range. Previously, receiving equipment for the VHF-UHF portion of the spectrum had been very complicated and expensive. The problems were worse in the beginning when vacuum tube technology was all that was available. It is a credit to manufacturing engineers that eventually the problem of building tuners was solved. As it turned out, the tuner became the least expensive and least troublesome part of a television receiver. After transistors came into use, even more reliable and compact designs came forth.

As early as the middle and late 1920s limited television demonstrations were being given in East coast cities, all using some version of the mechanical scanning system. By 1939 fully electronic television had emerged as the preferred system and it was possible to hold demonstrations on a much larger scale (photo 11.1). In December 1937 the Radio Manufacturers Association had agreed on standards for all electronic, monochrome television, and these standards had been approved by the FCC. At the New York and San Francisco World Fairs of 1939 closed-circuit television pictures of high quality were shown. Cameras picked up scenes outside the exhibit buildings, which could be seen on monitors inside the building. These, of course, were black and white images. Showing a good monochrome image was so impressive that no one thought much about color. The fair demonstrations were a big attraction as few people outside of the metropolitan areas had ever seen a TV picture. At the New York exhibition David Sarnoff stood before a television camera on April 20, 1939, and declared as follows:

> Today we are on the eve of launching a new industry, based on imagination, on scientific research and accomplishment.... . *Now we add radio sight to sound.* It is with a feeling of humbleness that I come to the moment of announcing the birth in this country of a new art so important in its implications that it is bound to affect all society. It is an art which shines like a torch of hope in a troubled world.... . It is a creative force which we must learn to utilize for the benefit of all mankind.

A feature story in *Life* magazine, June 5, 1939, reported the first U.S. telecast of a sporting event. It was a baseball game between Princeton and Columbia University, played at Columbia's Baker Field before 400 spectators. Princeton won 2–1. The video signal from the field camera was transmitted to the eighty-fifth floor of the Empire State Building and then retransmitted to an estimated 5,000 viewers in the Manhattan area. The received picture was described as rather fuzzy and indistinct. The camera then in use could not follow the ball, or bring pitcher and catcher in view at the same time. Despite the marginal quality of the demonstration, *Life* predicted that within 10 years audiences of 10 million viewers would be watching televised sporting events. This, taken in hindsight, turned out to be a pretty accurate prediction.

Progress in television was virtually brought to a standstill during the years of the war emergency. After 1945 technical improvements came rapidly, and America's love affair with TV commenced in earnest.

In the years following World War II one of the first television sets immediately

11.1 Television demonstrations at the San Francisco World's Fair in 1939 were for most fair visitors a first look at a live television picture (photo by Lewis Coe).

affordable to the average family was the Pilot three inch round tube model. Even with this minuscule picture the sets were viewed with delight (photo 11.2). Gradually, picture tubes got larger, but they were still round. It was like looking into the business end of an automatic washing machine. Finally somebody said, "Why are we watching round pictures when in the real world pictures are rectangular?" Of course, there were technical problems that kept picture tubes round. Eventually, these problems were solved and in 1949 the first 12x16 inch rectangular tube appeared. Round tube sets immediately became artifacts of the past and today you would have to search long and hard to find one for a collection.

The emergence of video recording equipment in 1956 pretty well ended the days of real time, live studio performances in which actors had to hope for letter-perfect delivery of their lines. Some of the horrendous bloopers that went on the air during the pretape days are still remembered with delight by older viewers. The first Ampex video recorders delivered to CBS in 1956 were large, very complex units using two inch wide tape. There were four recording heads spinning at high speed to scan the tape. They were called "quad" machines and cost $75,000 each. From that beginning we have evolved to the video cassette of today.

11.2. Pilot three inch TV receiver. One of the first affordable television sets for the average family (photo by Lewis Coe).

The first coast-to-coast network telecast by NBC took place on September 4, 1951. Meanwhile, work had been progressing on that impossible dream: color television. The old spinning disks were dragged out again by CBS and they managed to produce color pictures that were actually superior to those turned out by the electronic system of RCA. Forced to make a decision, the FCC approved the CBS system, even though it was recognized that it was a noncompatible system that would lock out all present owners of television receivers. This was not an astute decision by the FCC and even CBS did not actually push very hard to place their color system in operation. Meanwhile, RCA was convinced that only a fully compatible, all electronic system would be practical and so they continued their research to get the bugs out of their own system. In this they were finally successful. A chagrined FCC was compelled to reverse its former ruling and approved the new compatible black and white and color process on December 17, 1953. The adoption of the industry standard for a fully compatible black and white and color system was the beginning of color telecasting as we know it today. CBS had proposed skipping the black and white stage altogether and waiting until color was available. This would have resulted in no television at all until 1950.

The move to color came gradually, even after compatible standards were approved. Many small television stations could not immediately afford the change to color. The same held true for families that had just purchased a new black and white set. By 1968 color sets started to outsell black and white. After that date color sets dominated the market almost completely, even though black and white sets are still available today. Improved telephone company facilities made the first coast-to-coast color telecast possible on November 3, 1953.

The invention of magnetic tape recording of television signals in 1956 brought many changes in the industry. Almost everything that goes on public television today is taped in advance, even if the broadcast is to occur a few minutes later. One can appreciate the value of editing when, as sometimes happens, an unedited tape gets on the air!

News gathering techniques were significantly changed. The original process was to film remote scenes on 16 mm sound movie film. This film had to be brought by courier to the studio and developed. Then it was run through a scanner to convert it to a television picture. The first camera recorders were bulky and expensive. As the years passed, handheld camcorders could film a scene and then, by means of a satellite truck, transmit the pictures directly to the studio. The ultimate development of this system enabled television pictures to be sent directly from any part of the world. The first home recorders for television were monochrome units using ½ inch wide tape on reels. They appeared in the late 1960s. They were not equipped to record on-air television programs, having only a small camera for recording on tape. The tape could then be played back through a monitor. Other units intended for semi-professional use employed 1 inch wide tape. Color cameras for amateur use were so expensive that they were little used: a typical small color camera at that time might cost $5,000.

The development of video recording tape in cassette form led to the modern VCR, capable of recording off the air by means of a built-in tuner. Now camcorders using cassettes have steadily increased in capability, along with reductions in size and cost. The ability to film pictures in natural color with instant playback constitutes one of the great technical achievements of the twentieth century. Needless to say, the old home movie has practically disappeared. Many persons having 8 mm or 16 mm movie films they wish to preserve are having them transferred to video tape. Video cassettes were relatively expensive when they first appeared, yet there was still no comparison between a video cassette with 2 hours running time as against an 8mm movie film that only ran a few minutes.

The ultimate development in television will probably come when every home is served by a fiber-optic cable. Most experts feel that this is still many years away. Meanwhile, coaxial cable systems are operating in many locations.

Cable companies have been energetic in getting subscribers and offer their customers programs that cannot be seen over direct antenna reception. Viewers who live within 25 or 30 miles of a major city can usually have a choice of several free programs if they have a place to put up a suitable receiving antenna. Apartment dwellers, of course, do not usually have much choice but to subscribe to cable service if they want television. Cable distribution systems were originally used in mountainous areas where satisfactory reception could not be obtained with a simple home antenna. Now the cables are more of a public utility and have become popular with many viewers who are willing to pay for a greater choice of programs and better quality pictures.

As an alternative to coaxial cable distribution of television signals, considerable thought has been devoted to wireless systems where television programs are beamed to the homes of subscribers by high-frequency signals in the range of 27.5 to 29.5 GHz. As reported in *Popular Science* in November 1993, a company called CellularVision has been operating an experimental system in the Brighton Beach area of Brooklyn. In most cases the subscribers of this system have line-of-sight transmission of the signals. The signals can also be directed by simple reflectors to locations that otherwise would not be accessible. Subscribers have a choice of 50 channels at a cost of about $29.95 per month. This type of television distribution is best suited to metropolitan areas where hundreds of potential subscribers are located within line-of-sight distance from the transmitter.

Television network programs did not become possible until the telephone company perfected its coaxial cable and microwave systems. Television requires a wide-band channel to transmit the huge number of pulses required to transmit a picture, not to mention additional band width to transmit the FM audio signal. In addition to the microwave and coaxial cable channels, the telephone company facilities are now augmented with fiber-optic cables. These cables, using light beam transmission, have the wide-band characteristics that are needed to transmit pictures.

Even amateur radio operators now participate in television communication. On the high-frequency (HF) bands they must use a mode called slow scan television, or SSTV. In this mode only one image at a time can be transmitted. This is because television normally requires a wide-frequency band width that is not permitted on the HF frequencies. To use real time TV, the amateurs can use their 400 MHz band. This is normally limited to line-of-sight transmission. Under favorable propagation conditions, some outstanding distance records have been achieved. According to *Amateur Television Quarterly* published in 1995, a new record has been set with live amateur television between Columbus, Ohio, and Harrison, Arkansas, a distance of 628 miles.

It was recognized early that television had a great potential for educational uses. Many states have installed television networks linking universities so that resources can be shared. In Indiana one of the early networks linked Purdue with Indiana University and their branch campuses. By this method, students at branch campuses could take credit courses given at the main campus. For five years, starting in 1960, Indiana experimented with a television transmitter mounted in a large aircraft. By this means a widespread area could be covered with educational television. The excessive costs of this system could not be justified and it was decided the ground network linking the various schools was more economical.

Pirate, or illegal, broadcasting has normally been associated with voice and music transmission. Yet even television has had a few cases where persons thought they could play fast and loose with the regulations. In 1950 an outfit that should have known better, the Tube Division of Sylvania Electric Products of Emporium, Pennsylvania, was found to be retransmitting the television programs of WJAC-TV of Johnstown, Pennsylvania. It didn't take long for the FCC to hear of this little transgression and they acted promptly to close the station down.

Police Radio

The thought of a police car without radio seems rather quaint today, yet as recently as the 1930s that was the case. When a police officer went out on a call from a remote area, he was on his own unless he could locate a telephone. Today, officers stay in constant touch with their headquarters and can be confident that additional help will be sent if the individual officer needs it. In fact, it was not uncommon in small communities for the town marshall to not even have a car. He made his rounds on foot and got an occasional lift from a public-spirited citizen if he had to travel far.

Long before there was any thought that two-way communication with a police officer would eventually be possible, many types of improvised methods were used to contact the officers. In Galva, Illinois (population 2,800), during the 1930s, an ingenious method was used to notify the night officer that his services were needed. An employee at the city water plant, notified by telephone, operated the switch that controlled the town street lighting system. When the night officer saw the lights flashing he could make his way to the nearest telephone and call in. When the night employee at the water plant was terminated during the Depression, a new signaling system had to be devised. The solution was to place a loud buzzer on top of the telephone building that was centrally located in the business district. Here there was an operator on duty 24 hours a day and she could sound the buzzer when there was a call for the police.

Before there was any thought of two-way communication with police cars, a primitive wireless station had been set up on Catalina Island, off the California coast. This was in 1902, about 20 years before the telephone company set up a radio link to provide telephone service to the island. Prior to the coming of radio, crime had been a pretty safe proposition on Catalina. If the miscreants could get on board the next boat for the mainland they were safe from capture. The first wireless station of 1902 changed all this. Two men had held up the bar in the Hotel Metropole and got safely aboard a boat for the mainland leaving at 5 A.M. Unfortunately for the crooks, a message was flashed to the police on the mainland, who arranged a reception committee for the two when the boat docked in San Pedro.

The first tentative move in using radio for police purposes apparently came as early as 1921 when station WIL in St. Louis, Missouri, made a transmission to a police car. Comprehensive police communication systems didn't start to appear until almost a decade later. The reason for the delay in police radio systems was the fact that the entire art of mobile radio communication did not start to achieve a really practical state until the late 1920s. Installation of radio receivers in automobiles was originally for entertainment purposes. When efficient automobile receivers started to appear it became possible to use radio for police communications. Even though two-way communication with police cars was far in the future, many police agencies realized that radio would be very useful. Before communication with cars became practical, it was found that radio would be useful for communication between various fixed locations. In 1922 the Massachusetts State Constabulary began communicating between its various posts by radio, setting the pattern for state police agencies in the years to come. Until microwaves and teleprinter lines took over, state police radio telegraph nets operated to exchange data with other agencies over a wide area. These networks were operated by manual Morse code telegraphy and the operators were quite skilled in exchanging messages at high speed.

In 1933 a radio system was installed in Eastchester Township, New York, which permitted two-way communication between dispatcher and cars and from car to car. About the same time Bayonne, New Jersey, installed a radio communication system.

The first police radio systems were often one-way networks. The cars had receivers but no transmitters, so all that could be done was monitor the dispatcher's frequency. In turn, the dispatcher could not tell if a particular car had received the transmission. A car could respond by telephone when the opportunity came along, but generally the officer in the police car had to respond to the dispatcher's message and then handle the situation as best he could. It was quite common for the police dispatch frequency to be at the high-frequency end of the standard broadcast band. In Indiana the state police used 1,634 kHz as the dispatch frequency. This frequency could be tuned in on most of the broadcast receivers in the hands of the public. So the criminals could listen in if they wished and they probably did. The next step for this type of one-way system was to install a transmitter in the squad car so that it could respond to dispatched messages and call for help if need be.

By the mid–1930s most police departments were installing two-way radios in the cars. Many of these operated in the 30–40 MHz region. At this time the manufacture of a compact receiver for the high-frequency bands was still a difficult task. Many of the early two-way sets used what was called a superregenerative receiver. This was a simplified type of receiver that gave acceptable sensitivity with the minimum constructional difficulties. Although these receivers had acceptable sensitivity, they had little ability to reject interfering stations. The technology kept improving, and finally — within the limits imposed by vacuum tube design — some very efficient two-way sets were developed. These vacuum tube sets worked well enough but they constituted a heavy drain on the vehicle battery. With maybe 15 or 20 tubes in the transmitter and receiver plus a dynamotor for the transmitter, the total current drain when transmitting might be 25 or 30 amperes. Cars of this period were still using the 6 volt electrical system, which complicated the problem. It was quickly learned that with a radio-equipped police car it was not wise to have the radio on unless the engine was kept running.

As police use of radio communication continued to grow, it became necessary for police agencies to work out cooperative frequency usage plans. Most local police stations began to use the VHF frequencies around 150 MHz. This frequency band worked for short-range communications and, since the range was rather limited, the same frequencies could be reassigned in distant parts of the country. State police stations, normally having to cover much greater distances, were assigned frequencies in the 30 to 40 MHz range. These lower frequencies have occasionally resulted in serious interference from stations in distant parts of the country. Since there has always been a problem of police frequencies being heard outside of their designated service area, a solution was needed. It came in the form of the so-called PL (Private Line) equipment. In this system a subaudible tone is transmitted along with the regular voice signal. Only those receivers tuned to a particular tone will respond to the transmission. At one time it was common for police cars to respond to a call only to discover that it was a coincidence of car numbers and locations from another city.

The original FM police radios operated in what was termed wide-band FM. As the spectrum grew more crowded it was discovered that the band of frequencies occupied by an FM transmission could be reduced if only voice transmission was required. The band occupied by an FM signal is directly proportional to the modulating frequency. In voice transmission for communication purposes only about 3,000 hertz bandwidth is required. Fortunately, improved design of transmitters and receivers made a new narrow-band mode practical, and much frequency space was made available as a result. FM transmitters used in public broadcasting still use the wide-band mode to accommodate the wider range of frequencies needed for high-fidelity transmission of music.

The introduction of transistorized equipment ended the days of heavy battery drain from the radio. It also made possible more complex equipment without exceeding the space limitations of a squad car. Many departments adopted systems for transmitting data directly from headquarters to the car in the field. Secrecy of communications was a subject that received much attention. The early privacy systems were elemental and could easily be circumvented by scanner listeners with a low-cost converter. The later privacy devices employ the same digital technology used by the military. These devices are expensive and have not been adopted by all police departments. Most police cars monitor several adjoining services and the use of privacy devices blocks out this activity.

The matter of monitoring police radio by private citizens has always been a controversial subject. In some jurisdictions it is prohibited by law. This supposedly prevents criminals monitoring police activity to avoid apprehension. These kinds of laws seem to overlook the fact that criminals, being what they are, do not obey laws. There is no doubt that sophisticated criminal gangs can gain information of great value by monitoring the police. The great majority of criminal activity is probably not that well organized. In general, it is thought by many that police normally benefit from monitoring of their communications when it is done by responsible citizens. It often enables citizens to cooperate with the police by being aware of a specific situation. In addition, police benefit by the monitoring because it gives the citizenry a better appreciation of the good work performed by the police in protecting the community. Typically, however, scanners are becoming illegal in private automobiles unless the individual has specific exemption from the law. Amateur radio operators are normally exempt from such scanner laws because the legal amateur radio mobile equipment often is capable of receiving police frequencies.

Many state police radio systems have installed a system in which the squad car acts as a repeater station. In this way, when an officer leaves his car he takes a small handheld unit with him. The handheld unit sends and receives from the unit in the squad car. The officer is always in touch with his base, even though it be many miles away and beyond the normal range of a handheld radio. This method is very practical for the state police organizations that are normally covering a relatively large territory compared to municipal police.

Among the latest developments in police communications are the so-called trunking systems. These concentrate a number of users on a single repeater facility. Channels are automatically switched to the various users. Trunking conserves frequency space and enables users to have a better facility than they might be able to afford on their own.

Police scanners have undergone a great deal of development since the days when they were just a manually tuned receiver that was only roughly calibrated in frequency. The modern scanner searches dozens of channels automatically and stops when it hits an active transmission. A digital display shows the exact frequency being received. The channels can be programmed and stored in the memory. Scanners are now available to cover the entire range of VHF and UHF frequencies used by police, railroads, aircraft, and a multitude of other services. In the United States citizens have always had free access to the airwaves. The law does provide that private radio messages can not be divulged to anyone besides the addressee. As long as the listener does not tell anyone what he has heard, or use the information for his own advantage, he has not really broken the law. It should be noted that monitoring of cellular telephone channels is specifically prohibited by law.

Citizens of the United States are fortunate in this respect because in many other countries even the possession of radio receivers is regulated by law. The only way the telephone company can guarantee privacy of calls made over radio facilities is to go to digital encoded transmission. This would mean total replacement of the thousands of cellular telephones now in use, and that is not likely to happen soon. The only alternative would be to offer a higher-priced service with secure transmission, a service to which some users would probably subscribe.

Meanwhile, police are enthusiastic about the current surge in cellular telephone usage. It has put new radio-equipped cars in almost every section of public highway. Accidents are now reported within minutes and suspicious vehicles or persons can quickly be reported to the nearest police station. Before cellular phones came into widespread use it was necessary to find a public telephone to report any such occurrence on the highway.

Any discussion of police radio must surely include mention of the Motorola Company of Chicago. Look at any policeman's radio equipment — whether it is the speaker-mike on his shoulder epaulet, the Handie-Talkie on his belt, or the control box in his squad car — and you will likely see the ubiquitous Motorola "M" trademark. Motorola was founded in 1928 by Paul Galvin (1895–1959). Starting out on the proverbial shoestring, Galvin first purchased the rights to manufacture a device called an "A" eliminator. The first home radios were all battery operated and the eliminators were quite popular as they did away with the need for a bulky and messy 6 volt storage battery.

This was Galvin's first venture in manufacturing and it was not destined to last very long because home radios would soon be operated direct from the electric outlet. Next came manufacture of automobile radios and this was the field that established Motorola as a major manufacturer. The future of the company was assured when well-known auto manufacturing companies started equipping their vehicles with Motorola radios. From the car radio receivers it was a logical step to police radio, which eventually

12.1. Chassis of World War II "Handie-Talkie" showing compact construction using vacuum tubes (photo by Lewis Coe).

became a large part of the business. With the advent of World War II Motorola became a prime producer of military radio equipment. One of the first successful military products was the SCR-536 Handie-Talkie (photo 12.1) that went into full production in July 1941.

The SCR-536 was an outstanding example of clever design using more or less standard components that were not intended for miniaturization. All of the World War II radios were, of course, based on vacuum tubes: transistors hadn't been invented yet! The Handie-Talkie was a battery-operated transmitter and receiver contained in a case about 3 inches square and 12 inches long. Not exactly the kind of handheld radio that would be normal today, yet it was an outstanding development for its time. All of the components of a rather complex transmitter and receiver, together with the necessary batteries, had to be combined in the one small case. The tubes were of a subminiature type and the operating frequency was in the vicinity of 3–4 megacycles. A self-contained telescoping antenna was employed. The operating frequency was deliberately chosen to limit the range of the set, since it was intended to be used for short-range communication between troops operating within a small area.

America entered the war with surprisingly little modern state-of-the-art radio equipment for the armed forces. Much of it was really just modernized versions of World War I equipment. Nothing like the Handie-Talkie had existed before and communication between troops was limited to field telephones or flag signals. While the Handie-Talkies had a relatively short range, they filled a need for communication between ground combat troops. For longer-range communication Motorola also developed a walkie-talkie set. This was a larger set to be carried as a backpack with much longer range than the handheld radios.

Motorola today, through its subsidiary Iridium, is expecting to be active in the satellite wireless telephone service for which they have recently received an FCC license.

·13·

The Morse Code

The Morse code, which originally was devised by S. F. B. Morse for his system of land wire telegraphy, is one of those simple ideas that has outlasted its time. Early systems of telegraphy tried various methods to convey intelligence, most of them involving some type of visual display. Not until the time of Morse did anyone come up with the simple idea of assigning electrical pulses in the form of dots and dashes to represent the letters of the alphabet. Morse was not alone in this, as Steinheil in Germany and others elsewhere had similar ideas about the same time. Yet Morse's idea took hold and has survived since 1838. Morse, of course, used a visual display at first, in the form of the dots and dashes traced on a paper tape. Eventually, the operators learned to read the sound pattern of the register and the modern system of Morse telegraphy was born.

When Marconi worked to develop a means of radio communication, it was only natural that he used the Morse code as the means of signaling. Voice transmission by radio did not appear until after the turn of the century, and several years elapsed before it had much practical use. Meanwhile, the radio telegraph was king and the Morse code was what made it work. In the United States many of the first radio operators came from the ranks of land wire telegraphers and they used the American Morse code.

The army and navy were among the first large-scale users of radio and their people had for the most part been accustomed to using American Morse. With two codes in existence, American and International Morse, a chaotic situation soon developed. When one of the U.S. Navy ships tried to communicate with a European ship whose operators understood only International Morse, the results were not very satisfactory.

Finally, the War Department issued a circular on September 4, 1912, ending the confusion. Paragraph 3 of the order read thus: "The International Morse Code of Signals is hereby announced as the General Service Code of the Army and will hereafter be used for all visual signaling, radio telegraphy, and on cables using siphon recorders." Paragraph 4 then stated, "The

American Morse Code will be continued in use by the Army on telegraph lines, on short cables, and on field lines."

American Morse was Morse's original code and used dots and dashes, but there were spaced dots and dashes of different length. After ocean cables came into widespread use, the American Morse was found to be unsuitable for the characteristics of the original ocean cables. At an international conference in Berlin, held in 1851, revisions were made in the telegraphic code to eliminate the spaced dots and different length dashes. The result was called International Morse, or Continental Morse code.

This is the code used for radio communication and outside of the United States for land wire telegraphy as well. In the United States the original American Morse code continued in use for land wire telegraphy. Since most Morse land wire operation in the United States was phased out around 1950, there is virtually no use of the American Morse code at present, except by members of the Morse Telegraph Club who use it for traditional reasons.

The International Morse is now the worldwide standard for manual telegraph communication. Over the years this code has been used in every conceivable way to communicate. Light beam communication using the heliograph, naval searchlights, and various types of blinker lights all use the basic Morse. Even with all of its marvelous adaptability, the old code is becoming a thing of the past, and some classes of amateur radio licenses are already exempt from a code test.

Professional radio telegraph operators must still pass a code test to obtain a license, but this may change in a few years. Most modern ships, for example, depend on satellite radios for routine communications, and the Morse code radio telegraph equipment is mainly there as a backup for the newer methods of communication. Military radio operators are no longer trained in Morse code, except those who are assigned to special missions. The Coast Guard has discontinued the Morse code watch on 500 kHz, a practice dating from 1905. When the Coast Guard officially discontinued the use of Morse code in 1993, it was a sentimental occasion for some of the older personnel who had grown up with the old system of communication. As part of the closing ceremonies marking the occasion, a duplicate was transmitted of the first Morse message sent from Washington to Baltimore, May 24, 1844: "What hath God wrought!"

The Wheatstone system of high-speed telegraphy, originated by the British Post Office, employs punched paper tape for transmission and siphon recorders making an ink trace on paper tape for reception. This system is capable of speeds of 200 words, or more, per minute. On busy circuits the tape is split up between two or more operators so that the tape can be read as fast as it comes in. The tape is pulled along just above the operator's

13.1. International Morse Code, showing some of the unique dot-dash combinations used to send messages in other than English.

typewriter keyboard and controlled by a foot switch. The sending tape is punched in Morse code by a punching machine that is operated by a typewriter-style keyboard. When radio telegraphy came into use, the Wheatstone system was used for keying. It is still used where point-to-point radiotelegraph circuits are in operation. Operators become very adept at reading the receiving tape, or "slip" as it is called. They also are equally adept at reading the sending tape for checking purposes.

Morse's code was originally devised to send messages in the English language. It has, however, been adopted for almost all known languages. Special characters have been devised to send the special letters used in Spanish, German, Scandinavian, and Russian languages. Oriental languages posed a special problem. The Japanese solved it by adopting a simplified version of their ideograph characters. Known as Kana, the Japanese code consists of 48 symbols for the minimum number of ideographs needed to send a message. In Chinese the problem is not so simple. There was no way that code characters could be devised to send the hundreds of ideographs in the Chinese language. The Chinese must use a code book to send telegraph messages. These code books contain the ten thousand ideographs of the Chinese language and each one carries a four-digit number that can be transmitted by Morse. At the receiving office the numbers are translated by consulting the code book, and the original ideograph message can be reproduced.

Morse code was the backbone of most radio communication up until the time of World War II. Telegraphic communication can get through when voice doesn't. Furthermore, it can be effected with the very minimum of equipment. This was especially important for covert operations in the war zones. Starting in March 1942, the BBC began transmitting bulletins in Morse code for the Resistance fighters in Europe. This was apparently considered more effective than voice broadcasts. The resistance groups often had only very primitive receiving equipment. Also, it was thought that code broadcasts were less liable to be detected by the enemy than voice transmission.

Spies were landed in France by the Allied Powers, usually at night by light planes landing in secluded fields. Many of these spies were women and one qualification they had to possess was a skill in Morse code. Portable sending sets were reduced in size and weight so that they could be carried in ordinary suitcases without arousing suspicion.

If the spy managed to land in France and find a safe house undetected, the next step was to set up the portable transmitter and establish communication with England. The portable sets were necessarily of very low power, yet they had enough signal strength to reach the sensitive receivers listening for them. The Germans were aware of these activities, of course, and were constantly attempting to pinpoint the locations of the spy stations. With improved direction finding equipment they were often successful and caught many of the spies. Those that were caught were subjected to the tender ministrations of the SS: often they were sent to concentration camps and finally executed.

The enemy used spies with Morse code transmitters as well. One of the unusual stories of World War II, reported by *Life* magazine in 1945, involved movie actress Lucille Ball. It seems that whenever Miss Ball drove through Coldwater Canyon in Los Angeles, she could feel the buzz of Morse dots and dashes in one of her teeth. She reported this to the FBI. Sure enough, a few days later a Japanese spy was apprehended sending messages to an offshore submarine. It is presumed that Miss Ball had some bridgework in her mouth. This is about the only way such an incident could have occurred. Sometimes contact between dissimilar metals will detect radio waves.

When the Japanese overran the Philippines numerous American civilians and military personnel took to the jungle to operate as guerrilla forces during the Japanese occupation. These guerrilla forces had to improvise for everything they needed. But they managed to scrounge enough radio parts to build a makeshift transmitter. After many trials they managed to contact a commercial radio station on the California coast. They had some difficulty convincing the California·operators that they were indeed American guerrillas in the Philippines. Finally, by giving the correct answers to a series of questions they were established as genuine. The radio link thus established gave valuable information to the U.S. armed forces during the occupation.

When Herbert Yardley, the cryptographic expert, was working for Chiang Kai-shek in China before World War II, he professed to be surprised at the telegraphic skill of the Chinese. Yardley, who tended to be somewhat unflattering in his appraisals of the Chinese in other matters, was ready to concede that they did a good job as telegraphers. Yardley was in a position to be critical since he had been a Morse telegrapher as a youth in Worthington, Indiana.

In fact, his telegraphic skill enabled him to acquire his first job with the State Department in Washington. There he demonstrated an unusual skill in solving cipher messages and he soon established his reputation as a cryptographer. Telegraphic skill has always been regarded with awe by the general public. It is impressive to contemplate the ability of the human mind to absorb the telegraph code. When we watch a skilled operator sitting at a typewriter transcribing a steady stream of messages at 35–40 words per minute there seems to be no good explanation of how it can be done. Even more remarkable is the ability of many operators to use both codes, the American Morse and the Continental. They do this effortlessly and without confusing the words of the message. Telegraphy was one of the first white-collar jobs that was open to women. Women tended to excel at telegraphy and in general earned the same wages as men for similar work.

The secret, of course, is practice and more practice. The characters of the Morse code gradually embed themselves in the memory and from then on the operator is scarcely aware of any effort in reading the message. Ability to learn to telegraph varies with the individual, but few persons are unable to telegraph if they practice constantly. The time required may be as short as three or four months for persons having a special talent, and rarely will be it more than one year for others.

Many people were required to learn Morse code as part of their military training. However, many of these persons only learned enough code to qualify for a certain level. It is common to hear such persons say "I had to learn the code in the service but have long since forgotten it." In such cases all the person is saying is that he or she never really learned the code. Once it is really mastered it will not be forgotten, just as a person will not totally forget his native language.

Probably the code memorizing mechanism is similar to the process whereby music is memorized. Invariably, when telegraphy is depicted in the movies, what is heard is a meaningless gibberish of dots and dashes. With movie budgets in the millions of dollars it seems a pity that they can't afford a few dollars to hire a former telegrapher to send something that makes sense. One of the few exceptions is the 1941 movie *Western Union*, starring Randolph Scott and Robert Young. When the telegraph sounders are heard on the soundtrack of this movie they are sending real messages in Morse code.

The human skill that made the Morse telegraph such a successful system will probably never again be used in such a way. This is regrettable because the Morse system is so simple and uncomplicated that it is still one of the most practical communications systems ever devised. The main drawback is the three months to one year training period required before an operator feels comfortable with the process. No one now wants to put forth this kind of effort when other modes are available, even when the other modes require complex equipment that can easily become out of order.

When the Morse code was in regular use, it was quite common to hold contests to determine the highest speeds that an operator could attain. Two records that still stand and are listed in the *Guinness Book of Records* were made in International Morse code. On July 2, 1939, Ted McElroy received 75.2 words per minute in a tournament in Asheville, North Carolina. On November 9, 1942, Harry Turner of the U.S. Signal Corps transmitted at a rate of 175 symbols per minute using an ordinary hand key. This is about 35 words per minute. Allowing for the slower characteristics of International Morse, Turner's record is comparable to the 55 word per minute speed achieved by the old-time operators.

Prior to the invention of the so-called "bug" key in 1905, the only key in use was the hand key that hadn't changed much since the time of Morse. Since these records were established, persons have come forth claiming equal or greater speeds. However, Turner and McElroy's records are the only two currently on record as being performed before witnesses. Both men are dead now. McElroy was a professional radio operator who later went into business manufacturing telegraph apparatus. Turner was an old-time railroad telegrapher and amateur radio operator who served with the Signal Corps in the Pacific during World War II.

The wonder of the Morse code is its simplicity and adaptability to sending messages by a wide variety of means. The dot-dash code works well for all types of light beam communication, the most widely used of these being the heliograph. The heliograph used the reflected rays of the sun to direct a powerful beam to the distant station. Keying was accomplished either by tilting the reflecting mirror or using a small shutter that could be opened and closed to form the dots and dashes. Of course, the heliograph was limited to daytime signaling. Its range was determined primarily by the line of sight existing between stations and atmospheric conditions. Blinker lights and searchlight beams could be keyed in Morse code and used to communicate day or night. These light systems are still used in the marine service.

Blinker light systems were probably first used during the Civil War era. David Homer Bates in his book *Lincoln in the Telegraph Office* tells of the demonstration of light signals for President Lincoln. "Some one proposed that we should make a test of signaling at night by means of a calcium light, which could be displayed and screened at will by the use of a button, operated by hand, in the same manner as a telegraph key is manipulated; the alternate flashes of light, long or short, representing the dots and dashes of the Morse alphabet."

The demonstration took place on August 24, 1864, and messages were exchanged between the Soldiers Home and the Smithsonian Institution. Besides the president, the demonstration was witnessed by Joseph Henry, Rear Admiral Davis of the U.S. Navy, Colonel Nicodemus of the Signal Corps, and Colonel Dimmick of the U.S. Army.

Acetylene lamps were later used as an auxiliary to the heliograph that was adopted in 1877. Blinker light signaling did not play a large part in military signaling until after the invention of the incandescent electric light lamp around 1880. Then a variety of lamp signals were used by the world's military forces, including naval searchlights and small portable lamps used by the ground forces.

In emergencies Morse code signals have been sent by locomotive whistles. Experienced operators can communicate by tapping on tables with silverware or their finger tips. Morse has been used for flag signaling. A large flag is waved to the left for a dash and to the right for a dot. Perhaps the most unusual signals ever sent by Morse were transmitted by blinking eyelids. A prisoner was forced to appear on television, where he managed to blink his eyelids and sent the word "T-O-R-T-U-R-E." His captors did not realize what he was doing, but knowledgeable persons who were watching read the message.

Morse code is not usually associated with broadcasting, yet it has been used in emergencies. During the 1920s there were some severe weather emergencies caused by winter storms in the Midwest. At such times, communication was severely hampered because it depended entirely on open wire telephone and telegraph lines between major cities. In an effort to assist with the communication problem, broadcast stations started using telegraphic signals instead of their normal voice and music. The telegraphy was done by using audio oscillators to feed tone signals to the carrier wave being emitted.

The pioneer radio station of the University of Wisconsin was in operation as early as 1915. It did not have equipment for voice or music transmission, but sent Morse code weather bulletins for the benefit of local farmers. First licensed as 9XM, the station became a full-fledged broadcaster in 1922 with the call letters WHA.

When the Morse telegraph came into regular use, all sorts of abbreviations were devised to simplify informal communications by wire. The best known of these was the Phillips code used to shorten the time for transmitting lengthy press dispatches. The Phillips code was a lengthy list of abbreviations for common English words and phrases. Regular press operators had to be familiar with it in great detail. However, many of the words were picked up and used in everyday communication over the Morse wires. In addition to Phillips, the Morse telegraphers had a number list devised by Western Union, which assigned numbers to many common expressions.

When radio telegraphy came into use many of the old Morse expressions were continued. Today radio operators still use the number "73" from the old list, meaning "best regards"; "Hi" means laughter; "GM" and "GE" are commonly use for "good morning" and "good evening"; and "Fist" refers to the operator's sending style. Among radio operators the expression "OM" meaning "old man" is used as a salutation, even though the person addressed may be a teenager. Most of the common abbreviations are understood by operators of all nationalities, making it possible to exchange communications even if there is no common language between them.

•14•

The Vast Continent

William Crookes's "vast continent," which he was sure held the means for communication, is what we call the radio spectrum. The spectrum is one of the world's most valuable resources. Unlike the oceans, no nation can claim an exclusive section of it, yet all are free to use it. The allocation of frequencies in the spectrum is an example of how nations can work together for the common good when it is necessary. International radio treaties are among the most durable of such accords. The first of these treaties was negotiated in 1903 in Berlin, Germany, followed by another conference in 1906, also in Berlin.

Since then, over the years regular conferences have been held to bring radio regulations up to date. Even in war, nations have generally honored their treaties in reference to radio communication. It might seem that with the outbreak of war some nations would attempt to jam the enemy's radio circuits. Actually, this didn't seem to happen in World War II. It was apparently more profitable to monitor the enemy's circuits and hope to acquire useful information than it was to try and break them up. Most of the intentional jamming during World War II and the postwar period was done to international broadcasting. The communist countries were not anxious to have their citizens listening to propaganda from the free world.

Aside from propaganda broadcasts, deliberate jamming of the enemy's tactical communications in the field is considered a worthwhile countermeasure. Military suppliers have put considerable effort into developing suitable hardware to generate jamming signals to interfere with the enemy's voice and data circuits in the field.

Unlike other resources, the spectrum is invisible: you can't see it and it doesn't respect manmade boundaries. Yet it exists and must be handled in an orderly manner so that all may use it. The boundaries of the spectrum are determined by the natural laws of physics. The governing constant is the velocity of light waves, 300,000 kilometers per second. Specific spots in the spectrum are determined by the wavelength or frequency of the radio waves.

With the wavelength given, we can determine the frequency by dividing the wavelength in meters into the velocity. Thus a wavelength of 100 meters equals a frequency of 3,000 kHz. If the frequency is given, say 1,500 kHz, dividing this into 300,000 equals a wavelength of 200 meters.

The radio spectrum is usually considered to start around 10 kHz or 30,000 meters wavelength. This is about the longest wavelength that will readily propagate or radiate through space. From there it progresses downward to extremely shortwaves of centimeter length. Each part of the spectrum has its own peculiar propagation characteristics that determine how it is utilized for communication.

The low frequencies below 500 kHz, once the mainstay of all radio communication, might be assumed to be largely deserted with the general swing to high frequencies. This is not the case, however, and these old channels are throbbing with activity. Perhaps the most unusual is the use of low frequencies around 20 kHz by the navy for communication with submarines. The very low frequencies have the property of penetrating the ocean water and enable messages to be sent to submerged submarines. Previously, a submarine had to surface in order to receive radio signals from any great distance.

In 1958 Nicholas Christofilos, a U.S. nuclear scientist, suggested that extremely low-frequency waves might be used to communicate with the new nuclear submarines. The navy had long used low-frequency transmitters in the range of 20 kHz to communicate with subs. The low frequencies penetrated seawater better than any other radio waves. However, there was a limit of how deep the VLF signals (very low frequency) would penetrate. Christofilos's idea was to use extremely low frequencies (ELF) in the range of 30–300 Hz.

This was a startling concept and one not readily understood by engineers who were experienced in conventional radio transmission. It was known, of course, that frequencies as low as 10 kHz would propagate through space, given a big antenna and plenty of power. The ELF theory views the earth and the ionosphere above as sort of a giant wave guide in which the signals travel. The first step to implement this idea was Project Sanguine in 1969. The test site was near a northern Wisconsin town named Clam Lake. The location was chosen because it lay within what geologists call the Canadian Shield. This is a broad plateau of ancient dry granite that underlies half of Canada and parts of northern Wisconsin and Michigan. This type of soil was considered most favorable for transmission of the ELF signals.

Initial tests from Clam Lake were encouraging. However, the project ran into a snag that was political not technical. Residents of the area became alarmed with a project they didn't understand. In a rural area, talk of

extremely high power and antennas miles long soon had the locals convinced that they were being exposed to deadly danger. Public opinion
became aroused to the point where the navy found it expedient to shut
down the Clam Lake facility in 1977.

Finally, after overcoming local opposition, the project was revived in
1984. A new companion facility was erected at the K. I. Sawyer Air Force Base
near Republic, Michigan. The revised version links the Michigan transmitter with the existing one at Clam Lake. The antennas are supported on
wooden poles similar to electric power lines. Some short underground sections are used where it is necessary to cross roads and streams. The antennas are laid out in the shape of a cross to make them as omnidirectional as
possible. Total antenna length in Michigan is 56 miles. Clam Lake antennas are 28 miles in total length. Joined together, the overall antenna length
is 84 miles.

The present system is operational on a frequency of 76 Hz. Receivers
for this frequency are entirely different from those used on more conventional radio frequencies. Since the frequency is well within the range of most
good audio amplifiers, all that is really needed is a selective filter between
the audio amplifier and the antenna. One characteristic of this system is the
extremely low transmission speed. It is far too slow to transmit detailed
messages. Only a few code letters are transmitted, at a rate of around three
characters in five minutes, but this is enough to alert a submerged submarine to surface for two-way communication.

Since the reception is sometimes marginal, the messages are repeated
over and over. One of the ELF contractors is GTE, a company that runs the
system for the navy. One of their engineers once explained the technique as
follows: "It's like someone standing across a room whispering. At first you
can only hear part of what he's saying, but if he keeps repeating and repeating, eventually you can hear it all."

Heinrich Hertz once received a letter from a person who asked about
the possibilities of using Hertz's new waves for communication. For some
reason, Hertz construed the question as applying to low frequency waves,
what we now call ELF. He pointed out quite correctly that the antenna
required for effective radiation would be so large as to be impractical. The
following is a translation of the Hertz letter, written in 1899:

> Replying to your kind letter of 1st, I have pleasure in giving you the
> following particulars:
>   Magnetic lines of force may be propagated just as well as electric,
> as rays, if their vibrations are sufficiently rapid; in this case they pro-
> ceed together, and the rays and waves dealt with in my experiments
> could be designated magnetic as well as electric.
>   However, the vibrations of a Transformator or telegraph are far

too slow; take for example, a thousand in a second, which is a high figure, then the wavelength in the ether would be 300 kilometers, and the focal length of the mirror must be of the same magnitude. If you could construct a mirror as large as a continent, you might succeed with such experiments but it is impracticable to do anything with ordinary mirrors, as there would not be the least effect observable.

Hertz, with the basic tools for communication in his hands, seemed to be more absorbed with the scientific aspects of his discovery. Hertz could have hardly envisioned the developments that would come 100 years later. The idea of submarines roaming the world's oceans packed with deadly missiles and being controlled by the ELF system would have seemed fantastic. What was impractical in Hertz's time is still so today. The only difference is that now we are prepared to spend the astronomical sums of money required to turn the impractical into something practical, even though it has a very limited use.

A report to Congress by the secretary of defense in March 1994, which evaluated the continued need for the ELF communications system, concluded, "No alternative currently exists which can fulfill, as cost effectively, the capabilities afforded by ELF..." and "our review of ELF alternatives, costs and benefits indicates that ELF is the most cost effective means of meeting the full spectrum of communications requirements which will support optimum, unimpeded operations of our submarine force."

The main point of the protesters against ELF was that they feared the effects of the electromagnetic radiation from the high-powered antennas. It was claimed that such radiation might be harmful to both animals and humans. Studies were cited showing that humans living in the vicinity of high-tension power lines were showing a higher incidence of cancer. These studies were found to be flawed, however, because the people making them had never actually measured the levels of radiation involved. The public had been alarmed by some scare-type articles that had been published in the press. The power companies were alarmed too because their high-power 60 Hz lines were everywhere and if any bad effects were proved it would be disastrous for the utility companies. Most scientific studies seem to prove that radiation from power lines cannot be linked to cancer or other harmful effects. In fact, it is claimed that the earth's magnetic field is stronger than anything received from power lines. A survey of the published articles on the subject just doesn't seem to substantiate any cause for alarm from power-line radiation. In a study conducted in Finland it was reported that out of 135,000 children living within 500 meters of power lines, there were 140 cases of cancer. This was slightly less than the normal 145 cases that could be expected in a group of this size.

The navy has released figures showing that the magnetic field under the ELF antenna is 0.03 Gauss. This is way below the 3 Gauss maximum level recommended by the World Health Organization. The biological and ecological monitoring that has continued since 1982 has so far not disclosed any dangerous effects from the ELF operation. The National Academy of Sciences (NAS) has been conducting an intensive study covering the flora and fauna in the vicinity of the antennas. The final report from NAS is expected in 1996.

The effects of radiation of electromagnetic waves have never been exhaustively studied. Some authorities have claimed that dangerous radiation may be suffered even from the low-power transmitter involved in a handheld radio transmitter or a cellular telephone. A worthwhile field of study would be to gather data from the thousands of persons who have spent years working in high-powered radio stations. These people have received strong doses of radio energy for at least eight hours every working day. There are probably not as many people employed in this way now as there once were, but there are still thousands who spend their working days in a high-radiation environment. Studies of this group would show if there was any incidence toward cancer or other disease. The methods used in some of the surveys had no validity at all and one authority said it was analogous to judging the hazards of a nuclear plant by the number of carloads of fuel received in a day.

Another prominent user of the low-frequency end of the spectrum is the OMEGA long-range navigation system. Basically different from LORAN (Long-Range Navigation), it uses frequencies between 10 and 13 kHz. There are eight stations worldwide, including one in North Dakota. Each OMEGA station is a separate unit, and there are no master and slave stations. The stations use very high power and transmit a series of pulses on eight different frequencies. This is a slow-pulse system, contrasted with LORAN, and it requires 10 seconds to transmit the 8 pulses. From these pulses navigational information can be derived from as far away as 5,000 miles.

In addition to the uses for navigation, low frequencies below 100 kHz are still employed for worldwide communication, chiefly for messages to submarines. The U.S. Navy has several such stations, including NAA at Cutler, Maine, on 17.8 kHz; NPG/NLK at Jim Creek, Washington, on 18.6 kHz; NSS at Annapolis, Maryland, on 21.4 kHz; NBA at Balboa, Panama, on 24.0 kHz; and NPM in Hawaii on 26.1 kHz.

In addition to the fixed shore stations communicating with submarines, there are facilities for doing so on board large aircraft that serve as command centers. Typical planes are the Boeing E6A and the Lockheed EC-1300. These huge aircraft offer a practical platform for operating the VLF equipment. Incredible as it may seem, the antennas are in the form of a trailing wire, reeled out from the aircraft body. These trailing wires range in length from

4,000–26,000 feet long. The longer version of the trailing wire weighs around 2,000 pounds and constitutes a considerable drag on the aircraft.

When the aircraft supporting the wire flies in a tight circle, the wire tends to assume a near vertical position that is essential for best results. The normal patrol altitude of these planes is between 25,000 and 30,000 feet. By choosing the correct altitude they can deploy even the longest trailing antenna without ground interference. A submerged nuclear submarine has a considerable choice in means to communicate. It can receive signals from shore-based ELF and VLF stations, and from VLF transmitters on board command aircraft. It can release a special communications buoy that will come to the surface and flash a message via satellite. The submarine leaves the immediate area after releasing the buoy and the buoy automatically self-destructs after sending the message. In this way any enemy submarines in the area cannot easily determine the location of the submarine that sent the message. In addition to radio communication, the command aircraft can drop a sonar buoy in the vicinity of the submarine and use sonar signals for communication. The sonar buoy converts the sonar signals to FM radio, which is readily received on the aircraft.

Still another nonradio alternative is to use a blue-green laser beam projected from a satellite. The blue-green laser beam can penetrate seawater for a considerable depth and be keyed for communication. The exact depth of seawater penetration remains a classified secret at the present time. All these methods except VLF have very limited transmission capabilities and serve mainly to alert the submarine that more complete communication is needed. VLF can be keyed fast enough to operate teletypes aboard the submarine under suitable conditions. Submarines operating under the polar ice pack can surface through the ice and deploy antennas for conventional radio two-way communication. The broken ice fields confuse radar search operations and the communication antenna protruding through a hole in the ice is hard to spot by visual observation.

Trailing wire antennas are not new to aircraft. Comparatively short ones were used in the early days when operations were at frequencies too low to be radiated by antennas that could be mounted on the comparatively small aircraft of the period. Now, planes are large enough that antennas for conventional radio using the HF part of the spectrum can be mounted on the plane. Effective antennas for VLF are, of course, far too long to be mounted on any known aircraft, hence the trailing wires. The submarines also trail long wires for reception of ELF and VLF signals.

Another service currently utilizing the lower frequencies is the Coast Guard's LORAN system. Super power stations transmit coded pulses on 100 kHz (photos 14.1, 14.2). When received on the proper equipment, the seemingly meaningless pulses convey precise navigation information. Since

14.1. High power amplifier of LORAN transmitter at Dana, Indiana, puts out
pulses on 100 kHz with 400 kilowatt peak power (photo by Lewis Coe).

precise timing is the secret of this system, the stations use superaccurate
cesium clocks to time the pulses being sent out (photo 14.3). LORAN stations are grouped in chains, comprising a master and a number of slave stations. The master station for the Great Lakes chain is located at Dana, Indiana. This location was chosen not because of any strategic importance but
because a large tract of land was available under government ownership. It
was the location of the now closed Newport Army Ammunition Depot. The
slave stations associated with Dana are at Malone, Florida; Seneca, New
York; Baudett, Minnesota; and Boise City, Oklahoma.

Dana is manned by Coast Guard personnel 24 hours a day, 7 days a
week. The neat buildings convey an air of quiet efficiency in every detail. In
the control room are the cesium clocks that generate the accurate frequency
standard required. This timing is constantly monitored and corrections are
made if required. Timing is the heart of the LORAN system.

A complete signal at 100 kHz is generated in the control room. From
there the signal goes to the final amplifiers in another part of the building.
Here the water-cooled power amplifiers working at 22,000 volts generate
the 400 kilowatt peak pulse power required to cover the large Midwestern
area serviced by the chain. In the power amplifier area the visitor can almost
sense the terrific power being unleashed. In fact, some visitors may actually

14.2. Low-power section of LORAN transmitter at Dana, Indiana, generates the 100 kHz signal that feeds final amplifier (photo by Lewis Coe).

experience a slight headache as a result of the intense electromagnetic field. Station personnel are encouraged to wear protective aprons to shield against the X rays being generated.

From the power amplifier room a coaxial cable leads to the outside antenna. This is a vertical mast 600 feet high. Underneath the mast is a system of buried radial wires to act as a ground system. The tower is top loaded by a number of down wires at about a 60 degree angle. Even with the 600 feet height and the top loading, this mast is electrically short for 100 kHz or 3,000 meters. A truly resonant antenna would be ¼ wavelength or 750 meters (2,461 feet) high. It is obviously much more practical to use loading coils to make up for the shortage of tower height. All equipment in the station is provided in duplicate. This ensures continuity of the service as well as allowing needed maintenance work to be done. Two large diesel generators can operate the station for 30 days if needed due to loss of commercial power. These generators, either one capable of carrying the station load, start automatically if there is a power interruption and there is scarcely any break in the transmitted signals. All of these precautions are necessary due to the vital nature of the service. Aircraft and ships in a wide geographical area depend on the signal for their navigational information. If the master station is taken off the air due to some catastrophic failure, such as a loss of the antenna, other stations in the chain can take over the function of the master.

14.3. Cesium clocks provide time base for LORAN transmitter at Dana, Indiana (photo by Lewis Coe).

The LORAN system has been so successful and widely used both in the marine and aircraft field that is hard to picture it being discontinued. Yet the Coast Guard has talked of doing this very thing as a budget-cutting measure. Currently, it is costing about $300 million a year to furnish the LORAN service. The alternate system Global Positioning System (GPS) is costing around $400 million and critics say both systems are not needed. LORAN advocates point out that it is a civilian service, whereas GPS is basically a military system and can be shut down if the military should deem it necessary. With thousands of ships and aircraft equipped with LORAN, it seems that it must stay in service at least for another decade.

During the 1920s NAA, the old navy station at Arlington, Virginia, operating on 113 kHz, was a landmark for listeners with suitable receivers (photo 14.4). NAA was the first radio time signal to be broadcast, and standing by for the "time tick from Arlington" was the regular routine for most ship stations. The U.S. Naval Observatory was the source of the time signal broadcast from Arlington. Jewelers of that period often had special longwave receivers to take advantage of the time signal. Standard time signals are now broadcast on several frequencies by WWV, Fort Collins, Colorado.

From around 200 to 400 kHz the spectrum is pretty well occupied with aircraft beacons, marine beacons, and other navigational services. From 400 to 500 kHz the marine stations hold forth. The traditional calling and

14.4. One of the towers at NAA, Arlington, Virginia, about 1937 (photo by Lewis Coe).

distress frequency is 500 kHz. It is still used for that purpose although, officially, distress calls are now handled through an automated system working through satellites. One rationale for this new distress system is the capability to reach a ship anywhere on the world's oceans. With the old system it was sometimes difficult to communicate with ships in remote areas of the oceans.

The traditional AM broadcast band covers from 535 kHz to 1,605 kHz and one only need listen there to tell that it is intensively used. From 1,605 kHz to 30,000 kHz a wide variety of services occupies almost every channel. Included are marine communications, international broadcasting, amateur radio, military communications, and international aircraft flights. This frequency range provides short-, medium-, and long-range communications day or night. Frequencies above 30 MHz start to get into the line-of-sight category as they are not usually reflected from the ionosphere as are the lower frequencies. Above 30 MHz are found a wide variety of short-range services, including FM broadcasting, television, short-range marine channels, police and public service stations, amateur radio, and domestic aircraft. At the extreme high-frequency end of the spectrum are found telephone company cellular services, microwave relay stations, radar, and a wide variety of channels used to communicate with satellites orbiting above the earth.

The Radio Spectrum

ELF: Extremely low frequency, 30–300 Hz;
VLF: Very low frequency, below 30 kHz;
LF: Low frequency, 30–300 kHz;
MF: Medium frequency, 300–3,000 kHz;
HF: High frequency, 3,000–30,000 kHz;
VHF: Very high frequency, 30–300 MHz;
UHF: Ultra high frequency, 300–3,000 MHz;
SHF: Super high frequency, 3,000–30,000 MHz; and
EHF: Extremely high frequency, 30,000–300,000 MHz.

•15•

Radar

Unknown before World War II, radar today is one of the most important uses of the spectrum. The name Radar is an acronym derived from the phrase "Radio Detection and Ranging." It was officially adopted as a nonclassified description by the Office of Naval Operations on November 18, 1940. Modern radar is used in many ways: for navigation by ships and aircraft; by the military for locating the enemy and guiding missiles; by the police for catching speeders; and by the speeders for avoiding the police, to mention a few. Even in the time of Hertz it was known that radio waves would be reflected from solid objects but no practical use of the phenomena was envisioned for many years. In simple terms radar works by sending a radio signal toward a distant object, which is then reflected back to the point of origin. Since the speed of radio waves is known (300,000 kilometers per second), the distance can be calculated from the time required for the radio wave to make a round trip to the target.

Even though the basic idea sounds simple, the difficulty of designing practical equipment was enormous. The powerful transmitting pulse was sent out, then the sensitive receiver had to be turned on in time to hear the returning echo. This process had to be repeated at a high rate with the received echoes being traced on a cathode ray screen. In the United States much of the early fundamental research was carried out by a team of scientists at the Radiation Laboratory of the Masschussetts Institute of Technology. These men issued a series of 28 books detailing the basic principles of radar. These books from the Rad-Lab have become classics among electronic literature.

Writing in *The Electrical Experimenter* of August 1917, Nikola Tesla described with surprising accuracy the features of the military radar that came 25 years later:

> If we can shoot out a concentrated ray comprising a stream of
> minute electric charges vibrating electrically at tremendous fre-
> quency, say millions of cycles per second, and then intercept this ray,

after it has been reflected by a submarine hull for example, and cause this intercepted ray to illuminate a fluorescent screen (similar to the X-ray method) on the same or another ship, then our problem of locating the hidden submarine will have been solved. This electric ray would necessarily have to have an oscillation wave length extremely short and here is where the great problem presents itself, i.e., to be able to develop a sufficiently short wave length and a large amount of power… . The exploring ray could be flashed out inter-mittently and thus it would be possible to hurl forth a very formida-ble beam of pulsating electric energy.

The only flaw in Tesla's reasoning was that he expected the radio waves to penetrate seawater in detecting submerged submarines. It was found, of course, that radar will not penetrate seawater. Otherwise, Tesla's descrip-tion is a remarkably accurate account of the pulsed radar that was developed in the period before World War II. Perhaps the first practical application of this principle was in measuring the height of the ionosphere in 1925 by Gre-gory Breit and Merle Tuve of the Carnegie Institution in Washington, D.C. The methods pioneered by Breit and Tuve were adopted all over the world for measurement of ionosphere height. But it took another 10 years for the application of this principle to detection of aircraft and other objects. In England the work was accelerated by the realization that it might be the only defense against air attack by the increasingly hostile German Reich. Largely through the efforts of a Scottish scientist, R. A. Watson-Watt, the original British Home Chain of radar stations began to materialize.

The original British system worked on the comparatively low-frequency band between 22 and 28 MHz. This choice was made in view of the lack of suitable tubes to generate higher frequencies at the power levels required. In the words of Watson-Watt: "Throughout the whole of the development period the small team who was responsible ruthlessly sacrificed all refine-ments, elegances and versatilities in the desperate need for something to be going with. They never turned aside from their cult of the third best — 'The best never comes, the second best comes too late.'" This early British radar system with its obvious imperfections is credited with being the major fac-tor in winning the Battle of Britain.

Research continued in England and by 1940 the original radar chain was supplemented by the so-called CHL system (Chain Home Low), working on a frequency of 200 MHz. The British led the way in developing the cavity magnetron tube essential for generating the high frequencies required in radar. This was especially important for airborne equipment where the fre-quencies used had to be high enough to permit effective antennas on the planes. Late in 1939 the British had been able to start equipping their night fighter aircraft with AI (aircraft interception) equipment. Also, in March

1939 the first U.S. radar was installed on board the USS *New York*. It operated on 1.5 meters (200 MHz) and had a range of 8 miles. This radar set had been built by the Naval Research Laboratory in Washington, D.C., and tests were conducted during January, February, and March 1939.

By an extraordinary series of coincidences the Germans were unable to learn much about the early British radar installations. They knew, of course, that the British had erected a series of tall towers along their east coast. These towers had what were obviously radio antennas on them, but the Germans couldn't figure out what they were supposed to do. The first reports came from the crews of Lufthansa airplanes who dutifully reported them to the military command. Since a fast-flying airplane could not hover in one position long enough to take detailed measurements, it was finally decided that a fleet of air ships was the only answer to monitoring whatever was coming from those towers.

There was no way that a whole fleet of airships could be supplied, but the Germans did have the *Graf Zeppelin* that had been gathering dust in a hangar ever since the *Hindenberg* disaster in 1937. The old airship was renovated and made ready for flight again. Elaborate electronic equipment was placed on board and tested. Tragedy struck at one point when a technician fell to his death while trying to adjust an outboard antenna. Finally, on May 7, 1939, the airship set sail for England to learn the secret of those towers. When within 100 miles of the English coast, the ship was picked up by the British radar, which was working perfectly on that particular night. Now was the first of the extraordinary coincidences: the elaborate monitoring equipment on board the airship refused to work! The British were mystified by the radar blip they observed. It was the largest they had ever seen and was moving about 88 miles per hour. The poor Germans, flying in heavy fog, had no idea of their position and finally had no choice but to set a course for home.

On August 2, just before the blitzkrieg in Poland, the airship set forth once more. This time the electronic equipment was working perfectly. Then the second coincidence occurred. Believe it or not, on this particular night the whole British radar chain was not functioning. The Germans heard nothing and again returned home with nothing to show for their effort. In England the public was as ignorant as the Germans since the radar work was conducted in extreme secrecy.

Members of the local population around the Bawdsey Manor research station would sometimes try to sneak close to the station in the dead of night to try and find out what was going on. Some of these nighttime forays brought forth fantastic stories. Of these, "death rays" was a favorite. One local drove near the station and was confronted by a soldier on guard duty. The snooper panicked and tried to start his car. It wouldn't start and so he thought some mysterious power had disabled his engine. The soldier looked at his watch and advised waiting for 15 minutes. After waiting the prescribed time the car started easily. Nothing could convince the local that his car had not been immobilized by some mysterious force that was turned on and off on schedule. The obvious explanation was, of course, that in his excitement the man had flooded the carburetor. By waiting a few minutes the excess gasoline evaporated, enabling the car to start.

One wartime development that was widely publicized was the use of "chaff" or "window." This technique was devised to confuse German radar during Allied attacks. Thousands of strips of tinfoil were cut to the exact ½ wavelength dimension of the German radar frequency. When the strips were released in advance of the attacking planes, they gave 100 percent reflection of the German radar beams and made it impossible to aim anti-aircraft guns by means of radar. An amusing sidelight of this practice surfaced in the United States after the war when police started using radar guns in the active enforcement of speed laws. Uninformed individuals who had heard of the wartime use of chaff as a radar countermeasure thought the same idea would work for them. They soberly glued pieces of tinfoil on the front fenders of their cars. All they accomplished, of course, was to make their cars a better target for police radar beams!

Since the days of World War II the use of chaff as a countermeasure has continued. Carefully engineered dispensing systems have been developed for ships and aircraft. These dispensers enable the deployment of a large cloud of chaff to defeat the radar guidance systems of missiles and hostile aircraft. A ship, knowing of the approach of a missile, can deploy a cloud of chaff and take evasive action. Hopefully, the missile goes for the chaff and misses the ship. Combat aircraft are capable of using the same method to foil attack. Chaff dispensers have become very sophisticated. The most advanced models enable the operator to punch a button and automatically cut the chaff strips to an exact one-half wavelength of the enemy radar. This ensures maximum reflection of the radar beams. The chaff is stowed in long rope-like bundles. The machine automatically advances the "rope" and cuts off a bundle of the right length.

A standard practice during World War II was to equip lifeboats with radar reflectors that could be deployed to give a better target for rescue ships using radar to search for victims of sinkings. Some small U.S. companies had profitable contracts to produce these reflectors for the navy. The reflectors were arranged to open up like an umbrella and fold compactly for storage. Some were made of thin aluminum plates, while others, equally effective, were made of wire mesh.

Recognizing that the United States would in all likelihood be their active ally, the British were generous in sharing their radar information with the

Americans. Intense research efforts were being mounted in the United States to produce improved radar sets for their own armed forces. By the time of Pearl Harbor, the U.S. Army was taking delivery of the SCR-270 set, which operated on 106 MHz and had a reliable range of over 100 miles.

The story of that fateful day of December 7, 1941, and how the radar operators at Opana Point tried to alert the high command has been told many times. The SCR-270 was working perfectly and doing what it was supposed to do. Privates Lockard and Elliot were doing their job faithfully. That is where everything stopped functioning. The peacetime mind-set of the army and navy on Hawaii at that time just could not assimilate the possibility of enemy attack. It is thought that if the radar warning had been heeded, at least one hour would have been gained to prepare for the oncoming attack. Lockard and Elliott functioned at their level but they couldn't do anything by themselves. All the rest that were involved just didn't know what radar was, or what to do with it, and were still pursuing the Sunday morning routine of idyllic, peacetime Hawaii. An example of the peacetime mentality was seen in the attitude of the National Park Service (NPS) who had jurisdiction over much of the Hawaiian shoreline. The NPS was disturbed about the architecture of the proposed radar stations and said stiffly: "The Service will not depart from its standards." Perhaps most revealing was the comment by the young air force lieutenant who was on duty at the Information Center when Lockard tried to report the incoming planes. When asked after the attack what he was supposed to be doing at the Information Center, the lieutenant replied unabashedly, "Sir, I don't really know." Even though Lockard's devotion to duty did nothing to avert the Pearl Harbor disaster, he was later awarded the Distinguished Service Medal by Secretary of War Robert Patterson. Lockard received his medal on February 8, 1942, and was also given an appointment to the Officer Training School at Fort Monmouth, New Jersey.

Radar development has continued at a steady pace since the days of that SCR-270 at Pearl Harbor. During the Korean War, U.S. artillery units were equipped with the AN/MPQ-10 radar. This was a well-designed, microwave pulse radar on a mobile mount. Using it, the artillery could track incoming enemy artillery shells and mortar rounds. This information could then be given to the artillery batteries, enabling them to direct fire to the enemy gun positions. This equipment was so effective that occasionally it would detect small birds flying at a considerable distance from the radar. Sometimes the enemy was inconsiderate enough to fire directly at the radar set and it was not unknown to see radar dish antennas that had been punctured by shell fire from the enemy guns.

Before his death in 1937, Marconi had engaged in considerable research with microwave transmission. This work that had started as early as 1930 was ironic in a way because it marked a return to the part of the spectrum used in the very early research. Now, of course, Marconi had the advantage of vacuum tube equipment and a far more advanced technology. One of the first applications of the microwave experiments was the installation of a radio telephone link for the pope, between Vatican City and the pope's summer residence 15 miles away. In the course of the microwave research it had been noticed that an automobile passing through the path of the radio beam produced a noticeable change in the signal at the receiver. Marconi was quick to sense the military applications of such a phenomenon. The work was thereafter classified as secret. It is thought that if Marconi had been able to continue the research, the Italian Navy would have had first-class radar for the war in the Mediterranean.

When radar was first revealed it spawned talk of "death rays." This was a catchy term and appealed to the public imagination. The idea of being able to zap one's enemies instantly from a safe distance was very appealing. In the early 1930s the British government asked Watson-Watt if there was any possibility that radio could be used as a weapon. They were particularly interested in the idea of attacking airplanes. Watson-Watt told them that with the most powerful generator of radio waves that was then known they could not even expect to raise the blood temperature of an aircraft pilot as much as would result from a mild fever.

Thus the death ray idea died a quiet death. It was revived again when laser beams were invented. Even these concentrated beams have their limitations. To compete with conventional artillery or missiles, the laser beam requires generators so large as to be impractical. Whatever hazards we face as the end of the century approaches, it looks like death rays are not among them. The whole discussion of beam weapons recalls the occasion when a compressed air cannon was demonstrated for Napoléon Bonaparte. After a flawless demonstration, the emperor commented wryly: "Very impressive, unfortunately gunpowder was invented first!"

Before radar, much attention was paid to acoustic listening devices for detecting approaching aircraft. These employed exponential horns of rather large size. Electric listening elements were used and connected to sensitive amplifiers. These devices in their final form were quite efficient and could detect enemy aircraft at a considerable distance. About the time that acoustic listening devices were reaching a high stage of efficiency, another problem arose. Aircraft were flying faster than ever before. When aircraft approached the speed of sound the utility of the acoustic devices ended. The planes could be heard, but they were almost simultaneously arriving in the target area.

Even though acoustic devices soon outlived their usefulness for detecting approaching aircraft, there were other applications of acoustical devices that proved useful to the military. In 1945 the army had developed a high-power sound system known as "Polly." This system had four 500 watt amplifiers feeding a group of 9 horns. It could be airborne and was considered to be useful in addressing enemy troops with propaganda messages.

The system was recalled to duty during the Korean War. A dispatch in the *New York Times* of October 26, 1950, tells how it was used:

> With The Eighth Army, Korea, Oct. 25 — Two trucks loaded with North Korean soldiers were rolling toward the Manchurian border north of Anju when five United States planes came overhead. There was no rat-tat-tat of strafing guns and no bombs were dropped. The surprised Communists reached for their rifles as an unarmed C-47 came low and a Korean voice from the sky demanded their surrender, promising honorable treatment. Warning of annihilation from fighter craft if they refused to give up, the voice ordered the trucks to turn about. As the trucks began rolling back towards Anju, which was in American and British hands, the pilot observed other Korean soldiers filing from the hills and falling in behind the trucks. Soon a column of 300 to 500 Communist infantry was trudging behind the trucks.

Perhaps one of the most complex radar nets ever constructed was the Distant Early Warning (DEW) line across the Arctic regions. The construction, started in 1954, was designed to provide a chain of radar stations with the capability of detecting winged aircraft approaching the United States and Canada at any altitude. The line of radar stations extended from Cape Lisburne in western Alaska to Cape Dyer on Baffin Island in eastern Canada and was built in spite of some of the most severe weather conditions found in North America. Some of the sites were so remote that it was necessary to bring in heavy equipment by helicopter. In addition to the primary function of the radar, a complete communications system had to be built. It linked the stations on the chain with the North American Air Defense System headquarters at Colorado Springs, Colorado. Communications were accomplished using a combination of radio and landline circuits. The radio links employed a new technique known as "tropospheric scatter propagation." This system, using frequencies that had previously been considered useful only for line-of-sight paths, was found to be practical using special antennas and high power.

Tropo-scatter radio was found to be more economical than the microwave type of links that were the only other alternative. Called "White Alice," this over-the-horizon radio system also brought telephone service to many regions of the Far North that had never had it before. In many remote villages the only contact with the outside world was a conventional radio sending and receiving unit located at some central point in the community.

Once the stations were built they had to be staffed with operators who had been trained on the complex equipment they would be using. Not everyone was even interested in going to these remote polar regions. Those who did had to be trained because the duties were unique. For this purpose a complete DEW line radar station was set up in northern Illinois. With this training the new operators would find that everything looked familiar when they arrived at their Northern duty station. Nothing could prepare them for the severe weather they would encounter: subzero temperatures and winds blowing at 130 miles per hour across the icy wastes.

Unknown until the time of World War II, radar has emerged as one of the most useful applications of radio principles. The nation's air transportation system could hardly function without it. Ships at sea would have to go back to such early devices as foghorns and lighthouses for navigation under adverse conditions. Weather forecasting and storm warnings have achieved new levels of reliability due to advanced radar technology. Even the sports industry has started to utilize radar for timing the speed of baseballs and tennis balls. In 1974 Nolan Ryan threw a pitch that was clocked at 100.9 miles per hour. Tennis serves are now being clocked and the results displayed to the audience. Some critics say this practice has placed undue emphasis on power serves, compared with other aspects of the game. At the 1991 Wimbledon a player named Marc Rosset made a serve that clocked at 134 miles per hour.

A more frivolous use of radar is found today in the activities of electronic hobbyists. Small microwave oscillator units are available that transmit a signal on the frequency used by police radar. These little oscillators are mounted in a car and equipped with a pushbutton to activate the signal. Cruising along a busy highway, it is not hard to find some traffic moving at 75 mph or faster. The button is pushed and immediately all the cars equipped with radar detectors slow down to legal speed!

For those who are preoccupied with such matters, a complete printout listing every police radar in the United States is available from John Wilson (editor, USA Radar Directory, 6413 Bull Hill Road, Prince George, VA 23875, telephone 804-862-1262).

•16•

Collecting

Collecting in the field of radio is a hobby with unlimited ramifications. It can be followed by the poor man with few dollars and a very small house. The other extreme is the rich man with many dollars and a pole barn to house his treasures. Sooner or later, either rich or poor, the collector will wish for the pole barn, as things have a way of accumulating.

Ideally, the collector should be a person with some knowledge or interest in electronics. Very few old radios are acquired in good working order. Even those that work are likely to require replacement of certain parts and it certainly helps if the owner can do the work himself. A radio that is 50 years old begins to show its age. Capacitors dry out, resistors fail, insulation becomes brittle, and when these parts are suddenly hit with full operating voltage they will often fail in a rather dramatic way. Before powering up any old radio or other electrical device, a careful check of all the components is in order.

Specialized collections are always impressive. The new collector can choose from really old equipment dating from before 1920: battery-operated and AC sets from the pre-television era; small sets of colored plastic called catalins; table model sets called "cathedrals" or "tombstones"; and the early console models that were the predecessor of today's entertainment center. The console models are probably acquired the most reasonably. This is because a representative collection of console models requires a lot of space: you really need that pole barn (photo 16.1).

As might be expected, the 1920–era sets are expensive and hard to find in good condition. These are the radios first used to receive radio programs and they were built to look like electrical instruments, not pieces of furniture. The usual construction involved a Bakelite or hard rubber panel mounted on a cabinet of walnut or mahogany. They were carefully hand built by experienced craftsmen. These sets are, of course, all intended for operation on batteries. These were the radios bought by broadcast listeners who did not build their own and could afford the best. They date from the era when the prime object of listening was to see how far away you could hear something. Program content was of little importance to those early listeners.

Tubes for these sets are usually available as old stocks seem to keep turning up. Some ingenious solutions for replacing burned-out tubes have been devised. In one, a thin wafer fits over the prongs of the defunct tube. Transistor circuitry mounted on the wafer performs the same function as the previous tube. The burned out tube is left in place to preserve the original appearance and the transistors do the work. Other parts, especially dials, knobs, and other hardware of a proprietary nature may be very hard to find. For this reason, completeness is very important to the potential buyer and should have a direct effect on the price. One way to solve the parts problem is to locate a duplicate set that can be cannibalized for parts.

When more modern radios became available, many of the older sets were traded in on a new one. Dealers accumulated stocks of these beautiful old radios with their finely made hardwood cabinets. There was no market for the old sets and they could usually be had for the asking. Unfortunately, not many people were interested in them, and many just ended up on the junk pile. Home woodworkers often gathered up the cabinets to use the hardwood pieces for other projects.

Catalins and other small table model radios falling into the art deco class interest many collectors. A representative collection can be assembled in a relatively small space. These radios bridge the vacuum tube era to the era of transistors. They are found in infinite variety and some are quite rare and desirable, judging from the prices they bring.

The original radio manufacturers were often companies that had previously manufactured some type of electrical equipment. Others, hoping to cash in on the radio bonanza, simply hired an engineer to design a set and went to work. Some of the would-be manufacturers were deterred by the necessity of obtaining a license from the patent holders of the various radio circuits. It was virtually impossible to manufacture any radio that did not contain one or more patented features. In 1927 an RCA license cost a minimum of $100,000, quite a large sum for a beginning venture whose profits were by no means guaranteed.

Atwater Kent, one of the early manufacturers, was originally a manufacturer of automobile ignition systems. His uni-sparker ignition system became the protype of those used on almost all automobiles until the new electronic types took over. Kent was better equipped to enter the radio field than many of the others because he had extensive experience in electrical manufacturing, plus the know-how to do Bakelite molding of things like knobs and dials.

The sensitivity of the early Atwater Kent receivers could be greatly improved by adding a device called a variometer to produce regeneration. Kent didn't add these devices himself because he did not have a license from Westinghouse to use the regenerative circuit. Rather than risk being sued, he let the purchaser assume the responsibility of making the necessary changes in the circuit. In later sets the sensitivity was brought up to acceptable levels by the addition of tuned radio frequency amplifier stages. One of the first Atwater Kent sets mounted in a conventional cabinet was the Model 20. Instead of the Bakelite panels used on previous cabinet radios, the Model 20 featured a metal panel, finished in crinkle finish. This set still had three dials for tuning, but turned out to be very popular. Later this set was modified for single dial tuning and known as Model 30, which was introduced in April 1926.

Besides ignition systems and radios, Kent manufactured other devices, including sewing machine motors and other small electric motors. He even made a small intercom type of telephone instrument mounted in an oak case.

His first radios utilizing the open "breadboard" type of construction were unique in appearance and are highly sought after today. The term breadboard comes from the days when any self-respecting kitchen had a wooden board for rolling out bread dough. Early set builders sometimes acquired the breadboard from the kitchen on which to mount their radio parts.

Atwater Kent refined the breadboard type of construction to a fine art. The mounting board was high-grade walnut or mahogany with a highly polished finish. The tuning elements and audio amplifier sections were mounted in round modules screwed down to the baseboard. All the tube socket shells and other metal work were lacquered brass. Knobs and dials were molded of a rich brown colored material. The total cosmetic effect was handsome, and the sets worked well too. Later Atwater Kent sets utilized conventional panel and cabinet construction, but the same high-quality workmanship and materials made them distinctive.

By the mid–1920s the public was becoming disenchanted with the battery-operated radios. Operation from regular house current was the new order of the day, but at first it was not easy to accomplish. The problem was that 60 hertz hum from the power supply was hard to eliminate from the audio output. Also, there was still a large section of the listening public that thought the tonal quality of the battery-operated receivers was better. In England, where radio progress was roughly parallel to that in the United States, the same transition from battery operation to house current supply was taking place. The English have always referred to their household electric supply as the "mains." Those who preferred the new sets were said to be "mains minded."

Atwater Kent introduced their first AC model in 1927, but only after RCA made the type 26 and 27 tubes available. These tubes, together with careful design, made it possible to offer an AC set that was free of annoying 60 hertz hum.

The Depression years saw the end of Atwater Kent. It was hard to maintain an acceptable standard of quality at Depression price levels. It also appeared that Kent himself was just tired of running a radio manufacturing company. The company closed its doors for good in 1936 and Kent retired to California. His personal fortune was intact and he easily adapted to a life of ease in Hollywood. He died in 1949. The radios he made are cherished by collectors today and priced generally far over the price they sold for when new.

In the early days of the broadcast boom, manufactured radios were relatively expensive. This is why many persons built their own sets, either from kits or from descriptions published in popular magazines such as *Radio News*. One man who was determined to build radios at a price that the public could afford was Powell Crosley, Jr., of Cincinnati, Ohio. His radios were plain, no-frills models that allowed the average family to enjoy the rapidly growing field of broadcast entertainment. Crosley was soon being called the "Henry Ford of radio." One of his lowest-priced sets was the one-tube "Crosley Pup." This little radio, designed only for headphone listening, originally sold for $10. Today they are a scarce collectible often selling for around $300. One of the unique features of many Crosley sets were the book-type tuning capacitors. Instead of the interleaved semicircular plates usually used, the book-type capacitor employed two plates hinged at one end to open and close like a book. The tuning dial actuated a cam mechanism that caused the book to open and close, thus varying the capacity. These were undoubtedly cheaper to manufacture than the conventional- style capacitor and contributed to the lower price of Crosley radios.

It should be mentioned that the capacity element of radios was referred to as a "condenser" in the early years. In relevant literature this caused some confusion because condensers were also used in steam engines. To clarify the difference the term "capacitor" was adopted for electrical terminology. Another Crosley feature on some models was the use of controlled regeneration or feedback to improve sensitivity. By using regeneration Crosley was able to offer a sensitive receiver at less cost than would be involved with a more conventional circuit. Like all regenerative receivers, these Crosley sets, if misadjusted, would go into oscillation. Then they became a miniature transmitter that created howls in neighboring receivers.

"Tombstones" and "cathedrals," so named because of their cabinet shapes, are very popular among collectors. They are table model sets of fairly modern design that operate on regular house current. In working order,

16.1. Philco "end table" radio found at a flea market (photo by Lewis Coe).

they are still perfectly usable. This, together with their size, makes them very desirable to today's collector. A representative collection can be kept in the average home without undue crowding.

Among the larger, console-style sets, those built by E. H. Scott occupy a distinguished position. They were built to high-quality standards, reminiscent of the Atwater Kents. One distinctive feature is the fully nickel-plated chassis.

Surplus military equipment has also become collectible. The important criteria here is to have equipment that is in as issued condition. Sets from World War I are getting hard to find today and constitute a real prize when located because they come from a period when radio was really in a very primitive state. Sets from World War II are still common, although it is becoming a little more difficult to find sets in as issued condition. All of these military radios, regardless of type, are good examples of equipment built to a performance standard rather than to be competitively priced.

Receiving sets of the 1920s and 1930s tended to be either regenerative-type circuits, or the tuned radio frequency type. Regenerative sets used the principle of feedback, as invented by De Forest and Armstrong, to achieve adequate sensitivity. The tuned radio frequency sets employed a number of amplifier stages tuned to the signal frequency. The problem with these tuned radio frequency sets was the tendency of the amplifier stages to break into oscillation. Several patented circuits were devised to prevent this, one of the best known being the *Neutrodyne* as invented by Hazeltine. The tuned radio frequency sets usually required three dials for tuning. This was a nuisance when changing stations.

Most owners kept charts showing the dial settings for each station that was regularly received. Later, when single dial tuning was perfected, it became possible for the first time to simply twist the tuning dial and discover what was coming in. The ultimate development came with the superheterodyne sets, which initially were very complicated and expensive. For this reason they were slow to penetrate the popular market. In a superheterodyne set the incoming signal beats with a local oscillator to create a difference frequency. The difference frequency is lower than the incoming carrier wave and lends itself to efficient amplification. The superheterodyne circuit is used in almost all radio receivers today and the cost and complexity associated with the early versions have been largely eliminated by advanced engineering.

All of the early radios — the crystal sets and one-tube models — were limited to headphone listening. There just wasn't enough audio power to drive a loudspeaker. Brandes, a prominent manufacturer of headphones, sought to make a virtue of headphone listening. One of their 1925 advertisements showed an elderly gentleman wearing Brandes headphones accompanied by copy reading, "Grandpa's in a world of his own." Modern radio listeners with their Walkman headsets probably feel the same way!

The first loudspeakers were merely scaled-up versions of the magnetic telephone receiver and were not very efficient. As vacuum tubes became more available and affordable, one- and two-stage audio amplifiers could be used and these gave loudspeaker volume. The first real improvement in loudspeakers came with the "dynamic" or "moving coil" type. As the name suggests, these speakers used a small coil, called a "voice coil," suspended in a strong magnetic field. The voice coil was attached to a paper cone. These speakers overcame the limitations of the magnetic type and quickly became standard. The first ones required a power source to create the magnetic field. Improved magnetic materials resulted in the modern type that uses a permanent magnet to create the necessary field for the voice coil. Until the late 1920s it was taken for granted that the loudspeaker was a separate item, to be located outside the radio proper. Now separate loudspeakers are normally only found as part of high-fidelity amplifying systems.

A necessary adjunct of all early radio receivers was some sort of external antenna. In the very early days, when the prime objective was to obtain distant reception, the desired antenna was a large outdoor affair, as high and as long as space permitted. This was in the day when the radios had limited sensitivity to weak signals and broadcast stations were not numerous. This meant that most listeners outside of metropolitan areas had to be able to receive over distances of 100 miles or more. The requirement for a good outdoor antenna diminished as radio set design progressed and broadcasters became more numerous.

The standard antenna wire for home radios was #7-22 bare copper wire. This wire had seven strands of #22 AWG copper wire. It was flexible and strong, well suited for the purpose, even though there were many other types of wire that would have served the purpose just about as well. For decades this was the wire carried in all radio, hardware, and other retail stores. If you asked for antenna wire this is what you received. Apparently, it all could be traced to Marconi's use of such wire at his pioneer Poldhu, Cornwall, station. Early experimenters felt that if it "was good enough for Marconi it is good enough for me." The custom continued for many years, until the need for outdoor receiving antennas disappeared.

The final evolution of the external antenna came when sets were equipped with a small hank of flexible antenna wire permanently attached to the back of the set. This flexible wire could be strung out on the floor near the radio and gave the extra pickup needed for weak signals. Finally, the sensitivity of the radios was increased to the point where an external antenna was not needed. Instead, a small loop antenna, usually mounted on the rear cover of the cabinet was used. Even these were finally superseded by small coil antennas on ferrite core material. All radios using the loop style of antenna will exhibit some directivity, especially when listening to a weak signal. This means that some improvement in reception can often be observed by changing the orientation of the radio cabinet.

As the sensitivity of radios increased, largely due to improved vacuum tubes, new methods of production could be adopted. With the old style of circuits using low-gain tubes, it was imperative to reduce circuit losses wherever possible. This meant wood and Bakelite or hard rubber construction. Wiring was often #12 square copper wire arranged in point-to-point fashion. This type of construction was not adapted to mass production. Sets were, for the most part, built individually by skilled technicians who made a fine art of bus-bar wiring and good soldering.

As improved tubes and other components came along, minor circuit losses were no longer important. This made possible the shift to metal chassis construction. This adopted the radio receiver to mass production. The chassis could be stamped out by the hundreds, each exactly alike. Many of the components were riveted or spot welded in place. The wiring didn't have to be low loss anymore, so ordinary insulated wire could be used in random arrangement. Best of all, the work could be done by unskilled persons after brief training. This had the effect of sharply reducing the price of radio receivers and for the first time radios became a consumer item that was

Top: 16.2. Zenith "Transoceanic" portable, one of the first all-wave portables; *bottom:* 16.3. RCA Radiola III-A, four-tube set sold in 1923 for $65. Today's price is around $100 (both photos by Lewis Coe).

16.4. Grebe CR-6, three tube receiver sold for $180 in 1919. Today it is a collector's prize valued at $500 or more (photo by Lewis Coe).

competitively priced for the popular market. The new circuits had so much gain that it was no longer necessary to worry about losses. Some circuits, in fact, had to be deliberately robbed of gain in order to be stable.

The so-called catalin radios started out as low-cost radios intended for auxiliary listening in the home. Now they are one of the hottest collectibles, some selling for hundreds of dollars. Catalin is a thermosetting plastic material sharing a common ancestry with Bakelite, that was first developed by Leo Baekeland in 1907. The material was soon being widely used in industry for many purposes. It was, of course, used for front panels and other parts in many of the early radios. Catalin is similar to Bakelite, and can be produced in clear form and dyed in different colors. It soon became popular as a cabinet material for small radios. Plastic as a cabinet material had many advantages. The initial dies and molds to produce plastic radio cabinets were quite expensive, but once that expense had been covered it was possible to make thousands of cabinets that were exactly alike in all critical dimensions. This facilitated low-cost mass production since there was no tedious fitting of metal chassis into wooden cabinets, which often varied slightly in dimensions. The bright colors of catalin were attractive to buyers as well.

Another radio that is collectible and popular today is the Zenith Transoceanic portable (photo 16.2). This was considered to be the ultimate in portables when it was first introduced. It was the first high-grade portable offering worldwide shortwave reception besides the standard broadcast band. Still wedded to vacuum tube technology, it was a heavy radio with its necessary complement of batteries. This radio received a lot of publicity and went on expeditions all over the world. First produced in 1941, production was halted in 1942 due to the war emergency. Production resumed after the war and continued into the 1950s. Then the radio declined in popularity due to the competition from lighter, more compact all-wave sets and the inept marketing program conducted by the Heath company that became a subsidiary of Zenith. A new book by John Bryant and Harold Cones tells the story of the Transoceanic in detail — *The Zenith Trans-Oceanic: The Royalty of Radios.*

Television has its collectors too, although the field is not as wide as radio. One example of an early TV that every collector feels the need to have is the Pilot, 3 inch, black and white set. It is hard to believe that anyone once stared in rapture at one of these things. It is true however, and the 3 inch was the first affordable set for the average family. Of course, 3 inch sets are still made, but now they are strictly portables for occasional use. For regular viewing today, no serious watcher would be content with less than a 19 inch color set. One of the 3 inch sets is a prime collectible today, not only because they were only marketed for a relatively short time and are thus rather rare, but because they cause a great deal of interest from younger people who have never seen one.

Another TV collectible that is prized by collectors is the Philco model called the Predicta. These are fairly modern sets with a good-sized picture tube. The unusual thing about them is the styling. The picture tube is mounted on top of the cabinet and completely in the open. This gives the set a most unusual appearance that has guaranteed its collector appeal. A lot of original research was involved in producing a picture tube that would be adaptable to this style of mounting.

The following is a list of radio manufacturers during the broadcast boom: A-C Dayton, Adams-Morgan, Air-Way, All American, American Bosch, Amrad, Apex, Atwater Kent, Bremer Tully, Browning-Drake, Brunswick, Clapp Eastham, Crosley, Cutting and Washington, Day-Fan, De Forest, Eagle, Eisemann, Erla, Eveready, Fada, Federal, Ferguson, Freed-Eisemann, Freshman, Garod, Gilfillan, Grebe, Howard, Jones, Jos. W., Jones, Lester L. Kellogg, Kennedy, King, Klitzen/Michigan, Kodel, Kolster, Leutz, Magnavox, Majestic, Marti, Midwest, Mu-Rad, Murdock, Music Master, Neutrowound, Operadio, Ozarka, Pfanstiehl, Philco, Pilot, Priess, RCA, Scott, Silver-Marshall, Slagle, Sleeper, Sonora, Sparton, Splitdorf, Steinite, Stewart-Warner, Thermiodyne, Thompson, R.E., Thorola, Tri-City, Tuska, C.D., Ware, Western Coil, Western Electric, Workrite, and Zenith.

Epilogue

Despite having been an eyewitness to the full development of radio communication as we know it today, this has been a frustrating book to write. It taxes the memory just to recall all the many ways that radio has been used since Marconi's great idea. The frustrating part comes when I realize that even as I write, new ideas and new uses are still being developed almost 100 years after the original concept. Twenty years ago we might have thought that radio had reached its full development, but that would have been a shortsighted assumption.

Wireless transmission of power remains the great dream, as much a dream as it was in Tesla's time. Yet, in another 100 years who knows? In 1895 who could have imagined live television from all parts of the globe, telephones in almost every automobile, or for that matter automobiles themselves?

The broadcast boom was one of the greatest manias to ever hit the United States. It introduced the miracle of radio to the masses and it did so before there were any identifiable stars of radio entertainment. Radio brought entertainment to millions, yet the real heroes were not the actors, musicians, and comedians. The real heroes were the engineers, the Hertzs, Teslas, Marconis, Armstrongs, and De Forests who took Maxwell's theories and created something practical with them.

Glossary

AC: Alternating current.
AM: Amplitude modulation in radio telephony where the signal amplitude varies in direct proportion to the speech or music level.
CW: Continuous wave as generated by a vacuum tube, arc, or alternator transmitter.
DC: Direct current.
ELF: Extremely low frequency.
FM: Frequency modulation in radio telephony where the signal frequency varies in direct proportion to the speech or music input.
GHz: One thousand megahertz.
Hertz: One cycle or complete reversal of current per second.
HF: High frequency.
kHz: One thousand hertz.
MF: Medium frequency.
MHz: One thousand kHz.
UHF: Ultra high frequency.
VHF: Very high frequency.
VLF: Very low frequency.

Appendices

Appendix 1: Biographies of Radio Pioneers in the United States

Alexanderson, Ernst Frederik Werner (1878–1975)

Born in Uppsala, Sweden. Educated at the Royal Institute of Technology, Stockholm, and Königliche Technische Hochschule in Berlin, Germany, he came to the United States in 1901, and was employed by General Electric Company in 1902 as a junior test engineer. Alexanderson advanced quickly through the ranks at General Electric and held many patents in the field of electric traction motors. He is best known today for his invention of the alternator that bears his name. It was one of the first generators of high-power radio frequency waves of a continuous nature as opposed to the damped waves produced by spark gap transmitters.

Armstrong, Edwin Howard (1890–1954)

Born in New York City. He received an electrical engineering degree from Columbia University in 1913, then held the rank of major, U.S. Signal Corps, in 1917–19. Armstrong had absolutely no fear of heights. His escapades climbing to the very top of the radio towers on the RCA building in New York brought the disapproval of David Sarnoff. Major inventions of Armstrong include the regenerative circuit 1912; the superheterodyne receiver 1918; the superregenerative circuit 1920; and he invented the frequency modulation system, FM, 1933. His claim to have invented the regenerative circuit brought him into a bitter controversy with Lee De Forest who claimed the same thing. The Supreme Court finally awarded the legal claim to the patent to De Forest. After the Supreme Court decision Armstrong appeared before the Institute of Radio Engineers and attempted to return the medal they had given him for the invention of regeneration.

President C. M. Jansky of the IRE told Armstrong:

Sixteen years ago you received from the Institute of Radio Engineers its Medal of Honor in recognition of your outstanding contributions to the radio art. Because of a chain of circumstances well known to many of us, you came to this convention with the intention of returning this medal to us. The impulse which prompted this decision on your part clearly demonstrates how deeply you feel your obligations to the Institute. The Board of Directors has been informed by me of your views to which it has given full and complete consideration. Major Armstrong, by unanimous opinion of the members of the Board, I have been directed to say to you:

First: That it is their belief that the Medal of Honor of the Institute was awarded to you by the Board with a citation of substantially the following import; namely,

"That the Medal of Honor be awarded Edwin Howard Armstrong for his engineering and scientific achievements in relation to regeneration and the generation of oscillations by vacuum tubes."

Second: That the present Board of Directors, with full consideration of the great value and outstanding quality of the original scientific work of yourself and of the present high esteem and repute in which you are held by the membership of the Institute and themselves, hereby strongly reaffirms the sense of what it believes to have been the original citation.

Beverage, Harold (1893–1993)

Beverage was educated at the University of Maine in 1915. He joined General Electric in 1916, then later joined RCA and became director of research in 1945. He received the IRE Medal of Honor in 1945, being best known for his development of the long-wire receiving antenna that was used for transatlantic radio circuits.

Colpitts, Edwin H. (1872–1949)

Colpitts was educated at Harvard with a B.A. in 1896. He became vice president of Bell Laboratories, 1933–37. He invented the push-pull amplifier in 1912, and in 1915 invented the oscillator circuit that bears his name. The basic difference between the Hartley and Colpitts oscillators is that the latter uses a capacity bridge across the tuning coil. Hartley used a direct tap on the tuning coil to achieve oscillation.

De Forest, Lee (1873–1961)

A gifted inventor who opened the door to modern radio with his invention of the audion tube in 1906, De Forest received a Ph.D. from Yale in 1899. He held over 300 patents covering all types of electrical communication, and invented the phonofilm sound movie system in 1927. In 1943 an RCA booklet entitled *Electronics in Industry* paid tribute to De Forest as follows:

When Dr. De Forest made the first electron tube he had in hand the missing link in a great sequence of elemental revolution in human history — something as wonderful as any of the great epochal discoveries in man's development such as the making of fire; of bronze; of iron; of the wheel; of sailing vessels; of the telescope and the microscope; of the application of steam, electricity and automotive power! The visible evidence is a still growing $6,000,000 a year electronics industry.

Elwell, Cyrus Frederick (1876–1963)

Born in Melbourne, Australia, Elwell came to the United States in 1902, determined to get an education in electrical engineering. He graduated from Stanford University in 1907. After working on electric furnace design, he entered the radio field when he was asked to test a radio telephone system using a spark transmitter, but he quickly determined that this would not work. Meanwhile, having heard of Poulsen's arc transmitter in Denmark, in 1909 he negotiated for the rights to use the Poulsen arc and brought the first one to the United States. Elwell's work was the foundation for the Federal Telegraph Company that manufactured and sold arc transmitters all over the world. After his work at Federal, Elwell went to England and started C. F. Elwell, Ltd. (Craven House, Kingsway, London WC2), a manufacturer of home radio receiving sets. Elwell's company went bankrupt in 1923, a victim of the slump in the economy that affected many British radio companies.

Farnsworth, Philo (1906–71)

A Utah farm boy who discovered the principles of electronic television while still in high school, he started college but was unable to finish due to financial problems. He secured basic patents that were so strong that RCA could not manufacture television sets without a license from Farnsworth.

Fessenden, Reginald Aubrey (1866–1932)

Educated at Trinity College School, Port Hope, Ontario, and Bishop's College, Lennoxville, Quebec, he arrived in New York in 1886 and worked for Thomas Edison. Fessenden taught at Purdue University in 1887 and later went to the university of Pittsburgh where he became associated with George Westinghouse. Fessenden was one of the first to exploit the use of continuous waves for radio transmission and was the original developer of the high-frequency alternator later made famous by Alexanderson. Fessenden's company, the National Electric Signalling Company, won the contract to install a 100 kilowatt rotary spark transmitter for the U.S. Navy at Arlington, Virginia. Completed in 1912, the Arlington station had an outstanding signal for the time.

Fuller, Leonard (1890–1987)

Educated at Stanford University, Fuller received Ph.D. in electrical engineering in 1919. He was the president of Federal Telegraph Company 1913–14. While at Federal he carried on where Elwell had left off in the development of the arc transmitter. His research made it possible to scale up the arc transmitter to any power that was needed. This resulted in the two 1,000 kilowatt arc transmitters being built for the U.S. Navy in Bordeaux, France, in 1918.

Hartley, R. V. L. (1888–1972)

Educated at the University of Utah, Hartley was a Rhodes Scholar at Oxford University 1910–13. After graduation he was a research engineer at Western Electric 1913–25, and then worked at Bell Laboratories 1925–50. He received the IRE medal of honor in 1946. Famous for the transmitter oscillator circuit invented in 1914 that bears his name, the Hartley oscillator was an important component of many early transmitters, both amateur and commercial.

Heising, R. A. (1888–1965)

Heising was a research engineer for Western Electric and the Bell System. He invented the constant current system for modulating carrier waves with voice and music. The Heising modulator was almost a standard on most of the early radio telephone transmitters. Heising was one of the group of Western Electric engineers who started to study all aspects of high-frequency radio communication in 1921.

Langmuir, Irving (1881–1957)

Langmuir was born in Brooklyn and graduated from the Columbia School of Mines in 1903 with a degree in metallurgical engineering. Later he received his Ph.D. in physical chemistry from the University of Göttingen, Germany. After returning to the United States, he taught for three years at the Stevens Institute of Technology in Hoboken, New Jersey, before joining General Electric in 1909. It was Langmuir's genius with vacuum tubes that improved the De Forest audion so that it could be used as an amplifier on the first transcontinental telephone line in 1915. Langmuir sought to patent his improvement of the audion, but after a lengthy court battle the Supreme Court turned down his patent, saying it was only a modification of De Forest's work. This court decision was hailed by many who felt that granting Langmuir and General Electric the patent would place them in a position to control electronic devices of all kinds. Langmuir won the Nobel Prize in chemistry in 1932 and served as president of the Institute of Radio Engineers in 1923.

Pratt, Haraden (1891–1969)

Pratt received a B.S. degree from the college of Mechanical and Electrical Engineering at the University of California in 1914. He joined Federal Telegraph as an assistant engineer in 1920 and played a prominent part in establishing the early Federal Telegraph stations in California, and then became vice president and chief engineer of Mackay Radio after I.T.&T. acquired Federal and Mackay in 1928. Pratt was a fellow and past president of Institute of Radio Engineers, along with the holder of several important patents in early radio and radio navigation systems for aircraft. He served as telecommunications adviser to President Truman 1951–53 and was director emeritus of the IEEE. Like Armstrong, Pratt had no fear of heights. He once climbed to the top of the tower at one of the Mackay coastal stations and stood upright on the 18 inch square top plate surveying the surrounding countryside. Another delight was short-circuiting fully charged high-voltage capacitors just to hear the sharp crack. This backfired once when the screwdriver he was using conducted the charge to his body, knocking him unconscious. Fortunately, he revived while being rushed to the hospital.

Squier, George O. (1865–1934)

Squier received a Ph.D. in electrical engineering from Johns Hopkins University in 1903. During the First World War he was a major general and chief signal officer in the U.S. Signal Corps in 1917. He invented "wired wireless" in which radio signals were carried along wire lines, and once wrote a letter of recommendation for Lee De Forest, who was trying to get a job with Marconi.

Appendix 2: Marconi's Yacht

In 1919 Marconi became interested in having his own yacht, both for entertaining in the grand manner and as a research vessel that could travel anywhere for wireless tests. Marconi had a great opportunity to see the social possibilities of such a vessel when he was a guest on board Sir Thomas Lipton's *Erin* in New York. In addition, he had once been given use of the vessel *Thistle* by Empress Eugénie, wife of Napoléon III.

Thus it was, that in 1919 he purchased from the British Admiralty a vessel that seemed to be ideally suited to his requirements. This yacht, originally named *Rovenska*, was once owned by Archduchess Maria Theresa of Austria. Commandeered by the British, the vessel had been used for war service in the North Sea. Renamed *Elettra*, the vessel served Marconi for many years as a floating laboratory. It also suited Marconi's need for social entertaining in the high society circles in which he moved.

The *Elettra* was built in Leith, Scotland, by builders Ramage and Ferguson and was completed in May 1904. It was a pretty impressive ship by any standard, and of a type that is rarely seen today. The principal dimensions were as follows: overall length 220 feet; length at waterline 198 feet; beam 27½ feet and draft 16½ feet; and registered tonnage 232 and gross tonnage 633. The yacht was equipped with a triple expansion steam engine having a nominal horsepower of 137 and indicated horsepower of 1,000. The high-, medium-, and low-pressure cylinders were of 16, 26, and 42 inches in diameter. The stroke was 27 inches. Steam was generated by two coal-fired boilers having a total grate surface of 95 square feet. The main boilers had a working pressure of 180 pounds per square inch. Speed was normally around 10 knots with the engine turning at 90 revolutions per minute. Coal consumption at cruising speed was around 12 tons per day and enough could be carried for 12 days steaming. The yacht also was equipped with sails, which augmented the performance during favorable conditions. As might be expected, the yacht was well equipped with state-of-the-art radio equipment. This included a continuous wave transmitter for use on telegraph or telephone, a main spark transmitter, and a smaller emergency spark transmitter. In addition to the normal receiving equipment, there was a radio direction finding set. The foregoing was the equipment used in the normal operation of the yacht. Marconi, of course, had on board at most times a wide variety of experimental apparatus.

Starting in 1920, Marconi's work with the new shortwave medium took him frequently to Cornwall. There the *Elettra* became a familiar sight along the ports and coves from Falmouth to Lands End. When not working, Marconi could enjoy parties both ashore and on board his and other yachts that gathered in the area. Even the super rich can no longer afford yachts like the *Elettra* with a crew of 30. The beautiful yacht, which the Italian poet d'Annunzio called the "great white bird," came to an ignominious end at the close of World War II. She ended up as a bombed-out hulk on the beach in Yugoslavian waters. There was little left to remind one of the halcyon days when she was a floating pleasure palace where members of royalty and government officials, including Mussolini, were Marconi's guests.

Appendix 3: Radio Organizations

American Radio Relay League
225 Main Street
Newington, CT 06111-1494

Antique Wireless Association
2 Walnut Place
Apalachin, NY 13732

Quarter Century Wireless
  Association
159 E. 16th Ave.
Eugene, OR 97401-4017
  (limited to amateur radio oper-
  tors with 25 years of experience)

Veteran Wireless Operators
  Association
46 Murdock Street
Fords, NJ 08863

Society of Wireless Pioneers
P.O. Box 86
Geyserville, CA 95441

Appendix 4: Radio Publications

CQ— The Radio Amateur's Journal
76 North Broadway
Hicksville, NY 11801-2953

Popular Communications
76 North Broadway
Hicksville, NY 11801-2953

Monitoring Times
Grove Enterprises
P.O. Box 98
Brasstown, NC 28902

QST— Official Journal
American Radio Relay League
225 Main Street
Newington, CT 06111-1494

Appendix 5: Federal Communications Commission

Washington, D.C.

Serial No. 13   January 9, 1942

Notice To All Amateur Licensees

On December 8, 1941 the Commission ordered (Order No. 87) the *immediate suspension* of all amateur radio operation in the continental United States, its territories and possessions except as may be authorized thereafter by the Commission. In a public notice of the same date to all amateur licensees, the Commission advised that where amateur radio operation is deemed to be required in connection with the National Defense, appropriate authorization to engage in such operation would be issued, but only upon application by a duly authorized federal, state, or local official made to the Defense Communications Board.

Numerous requests from proper officials have been received for authorization to permit certain designated amateur licensees to engage in radio operation in connection with National Defense. Many were approved by the Commission upon recommendation of the Defense Communications Board. However, in the light of events since December 8, 1941, and based upon military security requirements, the Defense Communications Board and the Commission, after thorough study and reconsideration of the entire problem, have decided that all amateur radio operation shall be suspended, and that all authorizations previously issued in accordance with Order No. 87 be cancelled.

Appendix 6: Federal Communications Commission 56928

Washington, D.C.

January 9, 1942

Order No. 87-A

At a session of the Federal Communications Commission held at its offices in Washington, D.C. on the eighth day of January 1942;

Whereas considerations of national defense require the complete cessation of all amateur radio operation;

IT IS ORDERED, That all special authorizations granted pursuant to Order No. 87 BE, AND THEY ARE HEREBY, CANCELLED.

By order of the Commission.

Federal Communications Commission

T. J. Slowie,
Secretary.

Appendix 7: Order Closing Amateur Radio Stations, April 1917

To all Radio Experimenters,

Sirs: By virtue of the authority given the President of the United States by an Act of Congress, approved August 13, 1912, entitled, "An Act to Regulate Radio Communication," and of all other authority vested in him, and in pursuance of an order issued by the President

of the United States, I hereby direct the immediate closing of all stations for radio communications, both transmitting and receiving, owned or operated by you. In order fully to carry this order into effect, I direct that the antenna and all aerial wires be immediately lowered to the ground, and that all radio apparatus both for transmitting and receiving be disconnected from both the antenna and ground circuits and that it otherwise be rendered inoperative both for transmitting and receiving any radio messages or signals, and that it so remain until this order is revoked. Immediate compliance with this order is insisted upon and will be strictly enforced. Please report on the enclosed blank your compliance with this order; a failure to return such blanks promptly will lead to a rigid investigation.
Lieutenant, U.S. Navy, District Communication Superintendent

Appendix 8: Phonetic Word List Used in Radiotelephony

A: ALPHA	J: JULIETT	S: SIERRA
B: BRAVO	K: KILO	T: TANGO
C: CHARLIE	L: LIMA	U: UNIFORM
D: DELTA	M: MIKE	V: VICTOR
E: ECHO	N: NOVEMBER	W: WHISKEY
F: FOXTROT	O: OSCAR	X: X-RAY
G: GOLF	P: PAPA	Y: YANKEE
H: HOTEL	Q: QUEBEC	Z: ZULU
I: INDIA	R: ROMEO	

Appendix 9: International "Q" Signals Used in Radiotelegraphy (A partial list)

QRL: Are you busy? I am busy.
QRM: Is my transmission being interfered with? Your transmission is being interfered with.
QRN: Are you troubled by static? I am troubled by static.
QRO: Shall I increase power? Increase power.
QRP: Shall I decrease power? Decrease power.
QRQ: Shall I send faster? Send faster.
QRS: Shall I send more slowly? Send more slowly.
QRT: Shall I stop sending? Stop sending.
QRU: Have you anything for me? I have nothing for you.
QRX: When will you call me again? I will call you again at ... hours on ... kHz.

QRZ: Who is calling me? You are being called by....
QSA: What is the strength of my signals? The strength of your signals is....
QSB: Are my signals fading? Your signals are fading.
QSL: Can you acknowledge receipt? I am acknowledging receipt.
QSY: Shall I change to transmission on another frequency? Change to trans-
    mission on another frequency.
QTH: What is your location? My location is....
QST: General call to all stations.

   (Note: when the above signals are sent with a question mark they ask
the question. Without a question mark the signals are a statement.)

Appendix 10: Radio Museums

AWA Electronic Communication Museum
Village Green, Rts. 5 and 20
Bloomfield, NY 14469
Telephone 716-657-6260

Pavek Museum of Broadcasting
3515 Raleigh Avenue
St. Louis Park, MN 55410-0030
Telephone 612-926-8198

Headquarters Museum, American Radio Relay League
225 Main Street
Newington, CT 06111

U.S. Army Communications-Electronics Museum
Kaplan Hall, Building 275
Fort Monmouth, NJ 07703

Smithsonian Institution
American History Building
Washington, DC 20560
   Inquire for current exhibits.

Microphone Museum: Robert Paquette
107 East National Ave.
Milwaukee, WI 53204
   Museum has over 1,000 different microphones as well as early broadcasting equipment. Open free to the public on weekdays 8:00 to 4:30.

Appendix 11: Citizens Band Frequencies

Channel No.	Frequency	Channel No.	Frequency
1	26.965	21	27.215
2	26.975	22	27.225
3	26.985	23	27.235
4	27.005	24	27.245
5	27.015	25	27.255
6	27.025	26	27.265
7	27.035	27	27.275
8	27.055	28	27.285
9*	27.065	29	27.295
10	27.075	30	27.305
11	27.085	31	27.315
12	27.105	32	27.325
13	27.115	33	27.335
14	27.125	34	27.345
15	27.135	35	27.355
16	27.155	36	27.365
17	27.165	37	27.375
18	27.175	38	27.385
19**	27.185	39	27.395
20	27.205	40	27.405

*Emergency channel
**Highway common channel

Select Bibliography

Aitken, Hugh G. J. *The Continuous Wave Technology and American Radio 1990–1932*. Princeton, NJ: Princeton University Press, 1985.

Aitken, Hugh G. J. *Syntony and Spark*. Princeton, NJ: Princeton University Press, 1976.

AT&T Bell Laboratories. *A History of Engineering and Science in the Bell System: 1925–1980*. New York, 1975.

Bates, David Homer. *Lincoln in the Telegraph Office*. New York: The Century Co., 1907.

Bernard, Josef. *The Cellular Connection*. Mendocino, CA: Quantum, 1987.

Brittain, James E. *Alexanderson*. Baltimore: Johns Hopkins University Press, 1992.

Bryant, John H., and Harold N. Cones. *The Zenith Trans-Oceanic: The Royalty of Radios*. West Chester, PA: Schiffer, 1995.

Carron, L. Peter, Jr. *Morse Code — The Essential Language*. Newington, CT: American Radio Relay League, 1991.

Cheney, Margaret. *Tesla — Man Out of Time*. Englewood Cliffs, NJ: Prentice-Hall, 1981.

Desoto, Clinton B. *Two Hundred Meters and Down: The Story of Amateur Radio*. West Hartford, CT: American Radio Relay League, 1936.

Dreher, Carl. *Sarnoff: An American Success*. New York: Quadrangle Books, 1977.

Fisher, David E. *A Race on the Edge of Time*. New York: McGraw-Hill, 1988.

Friedman, Richard S. *Advanced Technology Warfare*. New York: Harmony Books, 1985.

Givens, Bill. *Flying with Loran C*. Blue Ridge Summit, PA: TAB Books, 1985.

Green, Jonathon. *The A–Z of Nuclear Jargon*. London: Routledge and Kegan Paul, 1986.

Harlow, Alvin F. *Old Wires and New Waves*. New York: Appleton-Century, 1936.

Hecht, Jeff. *Beam Weapons: The Next Arms Race*. New York: Plenum, 1985.

Jolly, W. P. *Marconi*. New York: Stein and Day, 1972.

Klein, Maury. *Union Pacific: The Rebirth 1894–1969*. New York: Doubleday, 1989.

Leinwoll, Stanley. *From Spark to Satellite*. New York: Charles Scribner's Sons, 1979.

Lightbody, Andy. *Submarines: Hunter/Killers and Boomers*. New York: Beekman House, 1990.

Lewis, Tom. *Empire of the Air: The Men Who Made Radio.* New York: Harper-Collins, 1991.

Report of the Chief Signal Officer. Washington, DC: Government Printing Office, 1919. Reprint, New York: Arno, 1974.

Ridenour, Louis N. *Radar System Engineering.* New York: McGraw-Hill, 1947.

Watson-Watt, Sir Robert. *The Pulse of Radar.* New York: Dial, 1959.

Yardley, Herbert O. *The Chinese Black Chamber.* Boston: Houghton-Mifflin, 1983.

Yoder, Andrew. *Pirate Radio Stations.* Blue Ridge Summit, PA: TAB Books, 1990.

Index

Index